Th...
Maiden's Handbook

The Modern Maiden's Handbook

The Shameless Guide to Blameless Living

Nina de la Mer

Foreword by Julie Burchill

PORTICO

First published in the United Kingdom in 2007 by
Portico
10 Southcombe Street
London
W14 0RA

An imprint of Anova Books Company Ltd

ISBN 10: 1 90603 213 0
ISBN 13: 9781906032135

A CIP catalogue record for this book is available from the British Library.

10 9 8 7 6 5 4 3 2 1

Design by Georgina Hewitt
Reproduction by Rival Colour, London
Printed and bound by Qualibris, France

This book can be ordered direct from the publisher.
Contact the marketing department, but try your bookshop first.

www.anovabooks.com

CONTENTS

FOREWORD

In recent years, there has been an outbreak of shameless sucking-up to the sad old ways of sexism, which has taken the shape of women who have benefited from all the blessings feminism has wrestled from the hands of the patriarchy – divorce, abortion, equal pay, education – whining for the return of 'traditional roles'. As ludicrous and tragic as black people demanding the return of slavery on the grounds that at least they were 'looked after' then, such slugs are obviously neurotic, unorgasmic cretins woefully unable to deal with freedom, and thus should all be shipped back to the nineteen-fifties forthwith, where they could enjoy traditional roles to their sexless little hearts' content.

Moaning minnies duly dispatched, the rest of us can cosy up with a copy of the excellent wit and wisdom of Nina de la Mer's *The Modern Maiden's Handbook*, which, in the sparkiest, sparkliest prose possible, posits the notion that the only thing wrong with modern life is too little feminism rather than too much. Refreshingly, Ms de la Mer understands that looking on the bright side of life is not simple-minded, that a smile costs less than a frown and that being a misanthropic misery bucket doesn't make you a sensitive genius, but rather a highly avoidable bore. This book is the antithesis of the *Daily Mail* worldview, seeing the delight as well as the danger inherent in everything from reckless sex to binge-drinking, and emphasising the importance of taking liberties as well as precautions in all areas of life from work to play. Although modern to a T, this book has lots of time for the old rules

– albeit such carefully selected nuggets as 'It'll all come out in the wash', 'No use crying over spilt milk' and 'A little of what you fancy does you good.'

All of women's vital life issues are discussed: love and sex, work and career, and health and lifestyle. Instead of treating the reader with kid gloves on the thornier of these, we're treated to no-holds-barred advice on everything from abortion to lesbian affairs to snorting speed and Brazilian bikini waxes. All handled with refreshing honesty and lots of sassy humour, giving a kick up the bum to the lifestyle books and magazines that promise so much and deliver zilch.

And unlike the plethora of how-to-breathe-while-putting-one-foot-in-front-of-the-other tomes which various famous cry-babies are snapped snivelling over in rehab, this is not a self-help book. Rather, it is a help-yourself book, encouraging you to fill your plate from the groaning buffet of pleasures and endeavours the miraculous modern world has to offer – and to go back for seconds. As for the weirdos who don't want it – if you can't stand the heat, get back to the kitchen; we'll have your fun and freedom if you can't handle them. Better still, fuck off and let the rest of us get on with the euphoric, free-falling rollercoaster ride that is being a modern maiden.

Julie Burchill, 2007

INTRODUCTION
A First Word in Your Ear, My Dear

Listen up ladies, it's time! It's time to rip up *The Rules* book and grab the twenty-first century by the balls; it's time to say 'yes, yes, yes' when you feel you ought to say 'no'; and it's time to get ahead by taking liberties as well as taking precautions.

Want to know how? Let the 'Modern Maiden' show you the way. Don't fret, though. I've no intention of droning on about keeping fit to keep your man. And I'm not going to tell you to revamp your looks to get a date or change your personality to find a job. Instead, this book acknowledges the refreshing truth that nobody's perfect and that the occasional cock-up (pun intended) won't do you any harm ... as long as you have the courage of your convictions. In fact, I will go further and reassure you that it's only by making mistakes – by behaving less than perfectly – that you can get all you want out of your relationships, your job and your sex life.

If you need convincing that it's time for the rise of this 'Modern Maidenhood', then let's take a brief diversion to spend some time with the ghosts of womanhood past. In the course of the last fifty years we reinvented ourselves more times than Madonna in her heyday. We shagged our way through the Swinging Sixties supposedly emancipated by the pill and now, thanks Mum, we're left with a generation of men who turn into Mr Floppy at the mere mention of the word condom. Then came the Seventies and a beating of breasts and an unnecessary burning of bras (to be fair to our Seventies' sisters, there was no Agent Provocateur back then), leaving us running around in circles with the double whammy of career and motherhood. I can hardly bring myself to mention the 1980s, when power suits were de rigueur and our female icons looked like men. And last but not least came our big sister, the 1990s, when 'girl power' was as manufactured as the group that sang about it and in a fit of pre-millennial madness the lager-lout ladettes tried to beat men at their own (drinking) game(s) while pretending to enjoy their beautiful game (admit it, footy's fun but it was mainly about Beckham and co. and 22 lovely pairs of pins, no?).

Let's wave goodbye to these feminist and ladette legacies – with perfectly manicured hands, natch – and go out there flaunting our sassiness and savoir-faire to achieve our wildest (and wettest) dreams; let's consign the dating guides and self-help manuals that have gone before to the dustbin of history, and make the bold decision to feel good about ourselves and the way we live our lives; and finally, let's attempt to redefine what it is to be female today in the realms of home, work, love, and sex.

If you think the above sounds too weighty, then allow me to reassure you as to what this redefinition involves, with a brief look at some of the lessons for modern living you will learn from the pages of this book: how to achieve the ultimate binge drinking session and deal with the inevitable hangover; how to extol the virtues of maidenhood whilst partying like a girl from 'da hood'; and how, at the same time, you can enjoy a rep as the office square. But the most important lessons I will teach you are: how to be shameless, yet blameless; how to be laddy-like but ladylike (which have previously been believed to be mutually exclusive – the point is, we can be both); and how to push the boundaries while keeping your reputation intact – but most certainly not your cherry!

So, if you're sick of books and magazines that spout information about a world you don't recognise, then this saucy little number is the perfect antidote! In it you will find not only practical advice on everything from bad debts to being a 'good' mum, but also irreverent musings on the treatment of women and girls by today's media as well as in contemporary society. In a reversal of the bog-standard advice you get from the usual fodder, it's time to kick back your (high) heels and read on if you:

* Don't care if he's 'just not that into you'; you're not that into him either!
* Have always questioned why boys have cutely named genitals (willies) and we've been lumbered with boring old vaginas;
* Have higher aspirations for motherhood than being a 'yummy mummy' and getting back into your old skinny jeans within a month of giving birth;
* Don't break out in a sweat at the thought of breaking a few rules at work – you'll do whatever it takes to get that much-needed pay rise or promotion.

In short, this book is a survival guide for fun nights out, naughty nights in, and making it through a day at work … or a day off sick; it's a rabble-rouser for Modern Maidenhood and all that this entails; and it's a celebration of our inner hedonist, harlot and heartbreaker.

It's no more Ms Nice Girl – The Rules were made to be broken after all.

CHAPTER ONE
The Made-up Maiden

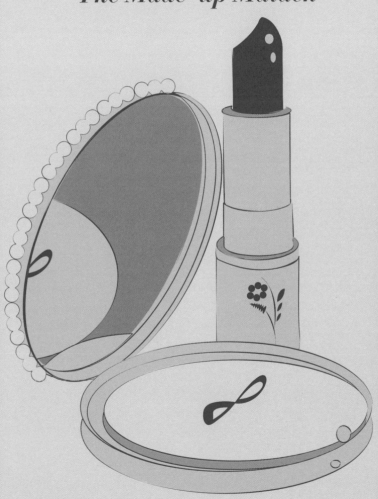

They say we are the fairer sex, and who am I to argue? Unfortunately, our prettiness comes at a cost and has resulted in the female of our species having to put in most of the (usually hair-free) legwork when it comes to the business of attracting a mate. Yes siree. Elsewhere in nature it is the boy who preens, plucks and pouts with great aplomb: consider the glorious peacock with his fanciful feathers, the colourful plumage he spreads in all its glory when trying to pull the right bird (ahem); the male eastern fence lizard who turns the skin on his throat and stomach a blue hue when the time is right for a bout of reptile romping; and not least, the efforts of the midshipman fish who croons a high frequency tune when some fishy fondling is the dish of the day. So many ways to send out the right signals …

The good news is we get our own back in the mortality stakes, with the human female usually outliving the male by several years (lifestyle permitting). In fact, both sexes can expect to live longer than ever before, and our chums in medical science are making such progress that by the time you've finished reading this book, your life expectancy will have increased by a good ten minutes. (Depending how quickly your read – if you skim it, chances are they'll only increase by an extra five, so it'll pay not to be lazy!) The bonus of this new-found longevity is that youth now stretches well beyond our teenage years and what we used to think of as middle age has shifted on a decade: our thirties are the new twenties; our forties the new thirties, and so on. A result for those who want to live out their lives as the good time disco diva with their hands (or legs) perpetually in the air; or for those who want to put off motherhood until they've climbed the career ladder or the highest heights of the Himalayas (or any other mountain, metaphorical or otherwise, you wish to climb).

Of course, every silver lining has a cloud, and this one's no exception. We may enjoy a healthier, fuller life with female life expectancy in the western world rising to an average ripe old age of eighty, but God forbid you should appear a day older than your actual number of years, (or have visible muffin tops, bingo wings or any other sign of, shall we say, maturing, which is more of a social faux pas nowadays than being sick out your nose and bum at a particularly formal dinner party). It's not as if our beauty demands stop there, for the Zeitgeist dictates (thanks Zeitgeist, I'll be having a word with you later) we have to feel as good as we look, as holistic therapies become ever more fashionable. You could say no (healing) stone should be left unturned when it comes to our beauty routines and no purse left un-emptied either.

Don't get me wrong. I ain't knocking the desire to look 'purdy', and this chapter's not about letting yourself go – and letting it all hang out – as feminist belief supposedly determines. Nor do I think that men and the media have conspired to make us hate our own self-image. Nope. We need to blow a lipsticked kiss of death to all of that prissy paranoia! There is evidence that the desire to look and feel good is not a modern manipulation, but rather dates back way before we knew our liposomes from our liposuction. For instance, the infamously glamorous Cleopatra didn't bathe in asses milk because she had a calcium deficiency – she wanted 'softer, younger looking skin'; Elizabeth I didn't whiten her face because she was auditioning for a role in a spooky ghost movie; rather, she was following the fashion of the time for that Vampish nearly dead look (and appropriately enough, many people did die from the practice of putting lead compounds on their face); and Plautus the ancient Roman didn't (somewhat misogynistically) write, 'A woman without paint is like food without salt', because women were hanging round the forum chucking cans of Dulux over their heads. Historians show us plainly (or rather, prettily), that beauty rituals and make-up have been around since 4000 BC the latter being worn in those times by both men and women alike. It would seem some people need a history lesson if they think the cosmetic companies alone have conspired to make us feel bad about not looking good.

It's sillier still to say that women are under pressure from men to be stick-thin and ever-alluring. Yeah, it's part of our natural make-up (ho ho) to want to radiate beauty in our attempts to attract a mate, but I think most of us know that once your man is hooked, he is exactly that. What's more, in a mini-survey I conducted of fifty women*, 32 per cent said they wanted to look good for themselves; another 40 per cent said they wanted to look good in front of other women; with only 26 per cent saying they tried to look good for the sake of men. And the other two per cent? Well, under 'other' someone said they wanted to look their best for their sister's husband (I know your type, lady, and we'll deal with you later!). Which all goes to show that women aren't being pressurised to buy make-up and the latest skin cream; we want to, nay, we enjoy doing it, and are, for the most part, aware that the expensive gloop of heaven in a little pot that promises to give you wrinkle-free skin simply smells divine and gives an air of glamour to your dressing table.

The problem is that things now seem to have gone that bit too far. Never before has the media and advertising bombardment been so insidious, so sophisticated, so ubiquitous. Not only do we have to look 'ten years younger' but we are told in an advert for *Pantene* that 'life makes your hair thin', and asked by a vitamin supplement firm, if we 'suffer from daily fatigue?' Ageing (a natural process!) may make your hair *thinner*, yes, but it's nothing to get worked up (in a lather) about. As for 'daily fatigue', again, yes, I am tired on a daily basis! Isn't everyone, from toddler to granny? That's why we humans are meant to get eight hours sleep a night, not stuff yet another chemically manufactured capsule of dubious worth down our gullets at the first yawn of the day.

* (if multinationals can get away with such an alarmingly small statistic to represent the effectiveness of their products, then so can your humble author)

I say it's time to strike a balance (or a pose – as you will) between the ludicrous claims from the cosmetic and advertising industries, the pressure from our partners, other women (and not least ourselves), and what we can realistically achieve with the body and face we've naturally been given. Let's relax about our looks and enjoy them as best we can (because God knows in another year you are going to worry about them even more!). To help you on your way, I've compiled a few useful hints and tips as to how you can cheat your way to gorgeousness, ignoring the myriad pressures from without and within. So, here, for your delectation, is the Modern Maiden's top to toe countdown to avoid pulchritudinous anxiety pangs.

Nine

Start a rumour in the office that the cute guy in sales has the hots for you. You'll be amazed how soon male competitiveness has everyone – cute guy included – thinking you're the bee's knees and asking you out on a date.

Eight

Give a wide berth to the women's 'glossies'. On page ten you will find an article on how to spot the signs of bulimia or anorexia in your mates, and on page eleven the latest fashions are modelled by pre-pubescent lollipop sticks. Why not get your fashion and beauty inspiration from the streets, old movies, your most glamorous aunt's wardrobe – anywhere but from these repetitive and formulaic magazines?

Seven

It's an old, yet gold, saying: 'Beauty is in the eye of the beholder.' You may think you look a knock-out having slathered on layer upon luscious layer of baby pink lip-gloss, but that bloke you are trying to impress might just think you've been eating a particularly greasy bag of chips. Take heart, fair maiden, one man's greasy chips is another's seductively slippery lips.

Six

Unless you are sixteen or under or have the grace and beauty of a super-model you are not going to pass muster in those high street store knock-offs of the season's must-have item. Okay, the article might be passable, but it's sure as Betsy not going to look genuine. The only women who get away with it, in a cruel post-modern twist of fate, are the ones who can afford the real thing. For the rest of us mere mortals, be warned!

Five

If your breasts are your *bête noire*, give them a boost by fair means or 'fowl'! Yes, rather than going down the invasive surgery route (more on this in the next chapter) you can buy a pair of plastic inserts to stuff down your bra that look rather like chicken fillets. Do remember to remove them if you are getting down to it after a hot date though, as you don't want your beau to think you've got a secret fried chicken fetish! And remember, most of us are wandering about in ill-fitting brassieres, so you may achieve the same effect simply by buying a good bra that fits properly and spare yourself this embarrassing denouement.

Four

Many articles on losing weight and dieting suggest sticking a photo on the fridge from the time in life when you'd eaten all the pies, as a motivational tool. My method is quite the reverse and so much more effective. Choose a favourite photo and stick it somewhere you'll often see. Thus, you will have a mental image of yourself at your most attractive and your high self-esteem will be contagious. The carrot, not the stick, will have you eating those carrot sticks!

Three

If your clothing size bothers you, or if you have one of those boyfriends obsessed with your being a certain clothing size, here is a handy tip for not feeling guilty or ashamed every time you open the wardrobe: in a clothing store, try on the size that you think will fit, not the size you want to be. Take home your glam garment, cut out the label and never think of the size again! Et voila! In spirit (if not in body) you can think of yourself as the perfect size for you!

Two

Never ever ask your mother if you have put on weight, or if that new haircut suits you. If we are own worst enemies when it comes to our looks, then our mothers are the evil mistress-mind behind that torturous self-doubt. From the first little pimple that they lovingly want to squeeze, to unhelpful comments about your wedding dress, it's best to keep quiet if you don't want to hear the worst.

One

The all-time number one winning hint for your future health and happiness is to adjust the dial on your bathroom scales to make them a few pounds (or kilos) kinder. For, in my experience, most women – no matter what their weight – wish they could shift that pesky last bit of bulge. If you're feeling really brave (the next chapter can wait five minutes) smash the hell out of the scales and lump 'em in the bin. *Now* a weight should have been lifted!

Well my pretties, it's clear as (a) mud (mask) that most of these tips are mind over matter. Indeed, you might think them daft. I'm not arguing … but certainly they are preferable to the lengths some of us go to in order to stay young and beautiful. In the next chapter, we'll take look at some of these desperate measures and how they are possibly best avoided.

Modern Dilemma

Dear Modern Maiden,

I've always tried to keep up with fashion but was shocked to find out recently just how far it now extends: on holiday in Ibiza two friends brought me up to date, bringing to attention my, what they named, 'unfashionably bushy' pubic triangle. Both had indulged in a 'Brazilian' bikini wax before the holiday and spent much of our time on the beach berating me for not having dealt with my own 'problem area' (their words)! I don't want to stick out like a sore thumb from the rest of womankind, but surely there's something slightly dodgy in becoming as hairless as I was, aged eleven? Aside from the aesthetic weirdness, I can't be bothered to add yet another treatment to my monthly beauty routine. Is it really so terrible to let it all hang out?

Yours confusedly, Ella

P.S. I pulled, they didn't. Ha!

Dear Ella,

Manicure and Pedicure. One hour each. Check. Facial. Forty-five minutes. Check. Leg wax. Half an hour. Check. Hairstyle and blow-dry. Yet another precious hour. Check. Add a Brazilian to this list and your purse will be a helluvalot lighter, and your lunchtime diary filled up from now until Christmas. (And it's only July.) So, there's one argument against giving into peer (or rather pubic) group pressure. If you'd like another, then think of how odd a shaved animal looks. So much prettier to be a cute little fur-ball, wouldn't you say? Besides – let's be blunt, pubic hair protects your private parts and it's simply much more hygienic to have it doing its job of catching drops of sweat. That's not to say a little trim wouldn't keep things tidy, as well as the muff police at bay in these times of waxed, epilated and shaven havens, but I can think of worse crimes in this day and age!

Yours happily hirsutely,

MM

CHAPTER TWO
The Ugly Face of Beauty

The expression 'putting your face on' (which originally simply meant applying make-up and thus changing your appearance) has never been more apt at a time when the rich and famous are quite literally peeling off their own faces and replacing them with new ones. Okay, okay, things haven't gone quite that far, but you get the impression that it's only a matter of time.[1] Certainly, in these days of fake tans and fake boobs, it wouldn't come as any surprise. What is surprising is that never before have so many people gone to such great lengths to mimic the prevailing look of the celebrity world, especially when we consider how absurdly contradictory this 'look' is: anorexically thin, but with giant, protruding (evenly sized) jugs – a look that appears more like a Barbie doll than the latest version of the toy itself does (it conversely has been redesigned to look more 'normal'). This figure is certainly unnatural for most of us and can be achieved by eating so little that your breasts go the way of your appetite (i.e. disappear), but then, since nobody nowadays (or so we're told) likes a flatter chest, having plastic surgery to regain your boobage is an increasingly popular choice ('In fact, why not go up a cup size or two while you're about it?' your plastic surgeon may casually ask, with dollar signs in his eyes).

History shows us that this is not the first time that thin has been 'in'. We need only look to the 1920s and the 1960s, when being boyish and skinny was the height of fashion. For, bizarrely, even though we all come in different shapes and sizes, perceptions of the ideal body shape follow the fashion of the times. Nowadays, more than ever, much like

1 With the exception of course of a certain world famous pop star whose face has already gone through more reincarnations than a Buddhist monk.

the vegetables at your local grocer's shop, we're rejected if don't confirm to the current acceptable version of the perfect figure (bear with me, I am going somewhere with this). I mean, take the humble carrot that is left to rot (or processed beyond all recognition in a TV dinner) if it has any knobbly bits or is not a uniform shape. Has society become so obsessed with perfection that normal gals will also be left on the metaphorical factory floor if we don't kowtow to the media's ide-alised notion of what it is to be beautiful?

Well, the answer, of course, is a big fat 'No'. Walk down any street and you will see variously – if you don't mind me continuing the fruit and veg metaphor – naturally whopping melons on gorgeous gals; petite celery-stick thin waifs; or the classically beautiful pear-shaped lass. The point being that, although some of us may aspire to fit into the prevailing look, few of us can achieve it.[2] But boy, we sure do put ourselves through the wringer trying. Let's now take a look at the things we get up to in our quests for the perfect physique, from diets to exercise, to the much talked about last resort of plastic surgery.

Fad Diets or F.A.D: **** ing Awful Deprivation

The promise of losing a stone in two weeks by trying out the latest fad diet is as irresistible to body-conscious birds as a cream bun is to the more corporally carefree among us. Yes, no matter how many doctors, dieticians, pleading partners and magazine articles tell us that crash dieting is not the answer to our weight 'problems', there's a moment in most girls' lives when we fancy shifting unwanted extra pounds quicker than you can say 'anorexia nervosa'. For, the time often comes, with the inevitability of the temperature reaching double figures at the end of spring, when we slip into our own double figures (of the stones, pounds and ounces variety) for the very first time, and drift from the

---

2 Or most of us, but it depends on which day of the week you've caught us as to whether we actually – yet more fruit and veg imagery, if you'll indulge me – give a fig.

carefree mini-skirted days of yoof into the muffin-topped, bingo-winged days of late youth (as I prefer to call my thirties) and beyond.

Your author, whose weight has yoyo-ed more than a gang of 1970s school kids, is now pleased to reveal the (dis)pleasures and the pitfalls of the more popular of these 'miracle' diets. Yes, as the old joke goes, I love dieting so much I go on more than one at once, so I am well qualified to provide you with the following mix and match daily menu from the latest weight loss regimes.

Breakfast

Let's start the day with the modern dieter's eating plan of choice:

The low-carb diet. Excellent. This means we can have a fry-up: bacon, sausage and egg. Hmm, no fried bread though, for the point of this diet is that you do not eat carbohydrates, as the body will use up more fat to compensate. A pity really, since carbs give us energy, help us sleep, and without them, a sandwich would be pretty boring! What's more, you might get into a state of ketosis if you don't eat them – an abnormal metabolic state which gives you bad breath, wind and nausea. How delightful. Perhaps not the diet to follow before a first date or job interview?

Mid-morning Snack

How about a diet created for people with low blood sugar (who are ill, not overweight, let me remind you)?:

Low GI. The basic premise of the diet is that you should eat foods that are low on the Glycaemic Index. Doing so helps to stabilise your glucose levels and slowly release sugar into the blood, thereby stopping snack pangs and making you feel full for longer. All very well if you can bear not to eat any sugar, and can be arsed to sort out which combinations of food to cook with which, and whether to boil or bake them (a potato, for instance, is high GI if baked, medium GI if boiled). But what's this? I can eat peanut butter to my heart's content. Yum-

yum. My favourite. Perhaps this dieting lark is not so difficult, after all.

Lunchtime

Well, a crash diet would not be a crash diet without the legendary **Cabbage soup diet** – yet another medical diet (supposedly) designed for clinically obese people who need to lose weight quickly in order to survive imminent operations. Eat cabbage soup and little else for seven days and guess what? Yup. You'll soon be skinny as a rake and be windier than a gale blowing in from the Atlantic. But even if it does the job, you should remember you will only be losing water, not body fat, and a cabbagey aroma reminiscent of old people's homes will waft about your house well beyond the duration of the diet itself. Hmm, I'm still full from my breakfast and snack. Think I'll skip lunch actually.

Dinner

The permadieters' diet of choice:

Weight Watchers. On the plus side with this 'eating plan' you can munch on anything you like. So, I'll be having my all-time favourite dinner: lobster to start, beef tagliatelle as a main course, and for dessert a perfectly sugar-coated crème brulée, all washed down with a half bottle of 2001 Pouilly Fumée. Oh, I seem to have forgotten the whole, um, 'point' to this diet, which is that each food has a points value based on saturated fat content, amount of fibre, and number of calories, and you can only eat a given number of points per day based on the amount of weight you need to lose. Whoops! I seem to have used up all my points for the week. Never mind. I can always suck on a lettuce leaf tomorrow.

What do you mean, I'm not allowed to mix and match diets? Well, it seems no sillier than going on one of these fad diets only to fall into your usual bad habits two weeks later. I mean, even your humble author who failed her basic physics knows it ain't rocket science – put too much in your mouth, don't expend enough energy and you will be Ms Lardy Lump, but eat well, and bust the occasional gut, and you'll be transformed into Miss Healthy Hotty. Your choice. And if you do eat a healthy balanced diet, there is nothing to stop you from having the occasional treat. But please do us all a favour and put the cabbage away.[3]

Gymboree?

For those of you who love your food and booze too much to even consider cutting back, pushing yourself to the limits of exercise is the best gym-shoed foot forward in order to achieve the body beautiful. The gym, for some, is like an addiction, and these endorphin enthusiasts embrace each new exercise craze, from good old-fashioned step classes, to spinning, to tae-bo, with ever-thinner and more toned arms. Of course, the real reason to indulge in these new trends is because exercise is so brain-numbingly boring that we need to find new activities to keep up our interest. Indeed, I am sure there are some who would try anything new that was going, and as such here are a few sporty suggestions you might want to put to your gym instructor.

Pi-ra-tes. (Same pronunciation as pilates.) This new class involves pilates moves but dressed in bandanas, brandishing the Jolly Roger and shouting 'land ahoy' for extra novelty value;

Tae-Chi-Chicken-Chow-Mein. An innovative new martial art designed for those who are short of time, combining the gentle skills of tai-chi while eating a Chinese takeaway;

Aero-bickers. Bouncing around with the usual aerobics steps, only you bring along someone you want to argue with and kick or punch them as hard as you can when the steps allow.

You get the picture. I am more of a gym fighter than a gym lover. If you want to know why, and you are a novice gym goer, allow me to explain: joining a gym can often be as bewildering an experience as landing on a different planet. The landscape you will encounter will be much like

3 Or at least save it until you need it when breastfeeding. See Chapter Four for more information.

an intergalactic space ship, with lots of shiny, unfathomable equipment. To make matters worse, you will stumble over (perhaps literally) instructors speaking in strange alien tongues which everyone else seems to understand[4] and bizarre lycra-clad extraterrestrial beings, perfectly toned and defined, the females indistinguishable from the males: nobody has any breasts. You may be left wondering where all the other first-timers are, the people who look like you (an ordinary Earthling). And then one day you will stumble on an aqua aerobics session. Here you will find the folks whose lack of co-ordination is matched only by their lack of desire to make a (flabby) arse of themselves in the more difficult exercise classes, so why not join in and take advantage of the fact that only your head will bob above the water, while the rest of your modesty is protected?

One thing is for sure, I would always recommend a trial run if your local gym offers it, for if in your heart of (lardy) hearts, you suspect it might not be for you, there's no point paying out for the joining fee and signing your life away for the next year. Besides, you could always take the easy option, and get an instant reward from your moolah, splashing out on a quick course of liposuction or a tummy tuck, as so many of us are apparently doing these days.

Plastic fantastic?

For, if we were to believe the media hype surrounding the boob jobs and the botch jobs of the cosmetic surgery industry, you'd think we were all at it, having our breasts augmented or reduced, our brows and vaginas tightened in order to cheat our way to perfection. Indeed, according to one survey consulted at the time of writing, over half of women aged 25 to 40 dream of doing just this and our newspapers delight in reporting a 'huge rise' in cosmetic surgery procedures. Let's take a closer look at these surgically enhanced figures, shall we? If we

---

4 Don't worry, as they'll translate 'grapevine', 'easy-walk' and 'box step' for you soon enough … then you'll be sure to wish they hadn't!

take the UK as our example, the 'huge rise' of 34 per cent in cosmetic procedures still only brings us up to 22,000 carried out in 2005. Quite a few you might think … hmm, let's get my calculator out to see what percentage of the UK population this is: 22,000 out of 60 million people – actually only about one in 3,000. Hardly an epidemic.[5] Besides, with most procedures costing about as much as a small car, it's unlikely the majority of us will ever afford one, or if we can, bother. (Spend that amount in the beauty salon and on new clothes and you'd surely see the same results.)

And yet, despite the horror stories and the costs involved, it's clear some of us would risk life and (with luck, cellulite-free) limb to go under the surgeon's knife. And why not, if your boobs are so big that you can't even bend over for a cup of coffee without knocking it flying, or more seriously, they give you a permanently aching back, or if your chest is so flat your boyfriend uses it as a tea tray. Don't forget though, these procedures can go seriously wrong, and you can end up with anything but the desired result – it's therefore very wise to check out your surgeon's credentials before going ahead, especially if you've chosen what's become known as a 'scalpel safari', or having cheaper surgery abroad.

Anyway, evolution will probably have a way to deal with such things that may frighten us all back to sanity. We need only remember that at the end of the Ice Age, when women greatly outnumbered men, we needed to compete harder in order to bag a bloke, at which point certain women evolved to have blonde hair and blue eyes to make them stand out from the crowd.[6] So, maybe in the future some of us will develop third breasts in order to compete with all the 36EE knockers, um, knocking around. And if that's not enough to put you off, well, all I can say is, I hope you enjoy the ride, my plastic princesses!

---

5 More significantly, 22,000 old people died in the UK from the cold in 2005 – which doesn't make for quite as sexy a statistic for a newspaper headline, does it?

6 Some would maintain this research is load of tosh, but hey, even in works of non-fiction we can use poetic licence!

Now, don't think my gentle mocking of exercise and dieting, and mistrust of the surgeon's knife mean I think we shouldn't try to stay fit and healthy. I'm not saying that instead of the recent much talked about trend toward 'raunch culture'[7] we should be piling on the pounds and trying to introduce 'paunch culture' as the norm instead. Indeed, in times of (some might say media-induced) worry about increasing levels of obesity, we probably shouldn't go down this route either. But, let's just try not to become obsessed with our (and other people's) bodies and enjoy the way we look. Let's also remember that body neurosis is an illness and, as most of us are already well aware, thinness does not equal happiness. In any case, who knows how long the thin look will be in? You never know! Curves could come back before the year is out and then what would we all do? Wander around with giant prosthetic arses (unless like your ample-bottomed author you are already 'blessed' with a J-Lo style big bum) or stuff big botty style chicken fillets down our trousers?

And it's not as if we did not have enough to worry about, with our internal female bits and bobs causing us no end of bother from the first day of our first period through to the menopause. As such, the next chapter is dedicated to our most private and precious parts which are such an, ahem, bloody nuisance throughout our lives.

7 As discussed in the hit cult book by Ariel Levy *Female Chauvinist Pigs. Woman and the Rise of Raunch Culture* (Free Press, 2005).

Modern Dilemma

Dear Modern Maiden,

My boyfriend has always been partial to big boobs and doesn't fail to hide his disappointment in my less than ample bosom. Throughout our two-year relationship he has strongly hinted that he would like me to have a breast augmentation but until now we have not been able to afford it. Having just got a healthy bonus in my last pay packet, I am considering getting the work done as a surprise for him. My concern is that having gifted him my big boobs, he may then start nagging me about my 'wonky hooter', another of his favourite topics of conversation. What do you think? Should I take the plunge?

Yours sincerely,

Sadie

Dear Sadie,

The only big thing you should contemplate in your life right now is the kick in the butt you give this less-than-charming man. I am not against plastic surgery per se, but the fact that you are being pressured into having this invasive procedure, rather than doing it for your own happiness, worries me. Your boyfriend's delight in knocking your knockers shows how shallow he is: does he want a girlfriend or a bra size? Some men use such put-downs as a means of keeping their girlfriends in check: they don't actually believe the insults they dish out, but it suits them to have a lover with low self-esteem. Others do so simply because they are nasty pieces of work. I don't know which is true in his case, but certainly I would not spend any of your hard-earned bonus on pleasing someone who seems to do so little to please you. Instead, I'd recommend using the bonus to treat yourself, so your self-esteem, not your cup-size, runneth over!

Yours small-but-perfectly-formed,

MM

Dear Modern Maiden,

I bought one of those celebrity fitness DVDs in the New Year. After doing it three times a week for six months, I still don't look like the 'celeb' on the front cover. Money back, or what?!

Yours dejectedly,

Isla

Dear Isla

Promises, promises. You have a baby and are finding those extra kilos hard to shift. Why not follow Celebrity X's 'Get Back into Shape Just Four Weeks After Giving Birth' DVD. Why not? 'Cause Celebrity X had a tummy tuck at the same time as her C-Section and hasn't stepped inside a gym for months, save for the action shots in the DVD. Or how about aerobicising your little socks off to the latest Z-list celebrity's 'Bikini Fit Not Wobbly Bits' home workout book? Well, I wouldn't bother – Ms Z List had liposuction and a double dose of botox before the promotional photos were taken. Bitter sarcasm aside, I understand your reasons for preferring to exercise at home. Indeed, there are many of us who would do all we can to avoid the ugly glare of the public eye while we sweat it out in a gym or as we puff our way around the local park. But next time you make such a purchase, you'll probably find fitness DVDs without a celebrity 'figurehead' come more highly recommended.

And to answer your question, no, I don't think you can ask for your money back if you don't look like the celeb on the front cover after all your hard work. But why would you want to look like somebody else anyway? I'd rather start trends than aspire to be a carbon copy of some past-it perma-tanned poseuse. Wouldn't you?

Yours individually,

MM

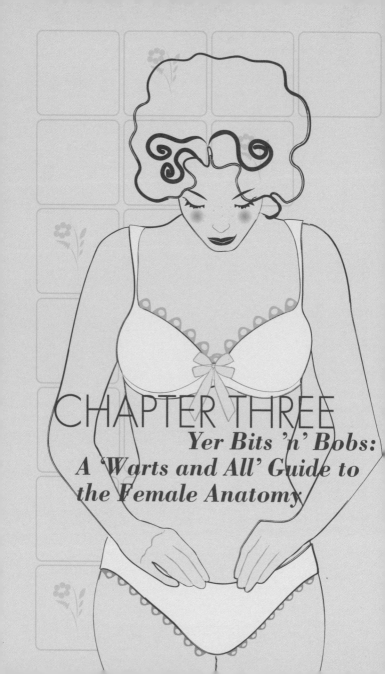

CHAPTER THREE

Yer Bits 'n' Bobs:
A 'Warts and All' Guide to
the Female Anatomy

Clichés usually have some basis in fact, and the following one rings truer than most, having left generations of parents (possibly including some of you) flapping like over-excited moths in a jam jar:
'Mum. Dad. Where *do* babies come from?'

Firstly there is the moral issue to confront, namely whether to waffle evasively about 'the stork' and 'mummy's tummy', or whether simply to come out with the plain, hard … facts, dears, facts! What did you think I was going to say? Which brings us to the perhaps more troubling linguistic problem of just how to describe the exact moment of being pushed out of our mother's, err … what shall we call it? Vagina? Too medical, too gynaecological! Fanny? Too comic, too bawdy! Pussy? Cunt? You've got to be kidding! We're trying to explain the precious moment of birth, not scripting an 'erotic' movie!

And if it's a little girl who comes into the world the situation is soon exacerbated when she starts potty training and her 'private parts' need to be identified. Because whilst little boys' penises are universally and affectionately known as 'willies', there isn't yet one familiar, friendly term for a female's genitals. This can lead to endless confusion among the children in the family. Take, for example, 'minky': in one family this may mean a vagina, but next door it's the name for a child's comfort toy. Imagine the scene:

Child one: 'I like your minky; can I play with it?'
Child two, clunking child one around the head: 'No! Mum says that's private!' 'Waaaaaaa!'

Enough, then, of this tongue-tied twaddle! Let's not beat around the bush any longer (never was a phrase so apt), and let's find instead a collective term of endearment for our most precious and private parts! Any ideas? Well, minky it is then, for now.

At the first major gynaecological hurdle in a girl's life, the opposite problem crops up, for no sooner does she start her period than she will have to endure the endless crude or euphemistic terms for her menstrual cycle. We all know and loathe such pathetic niceties as 'the time of the month', 'having the painters in', or the positively ancient 'the curse', which makes me wonder if it is possible that our period is still something to be ashamed of in this day and age? Why not simply tell it like it is, like the plain-speaking Australians who coined the delightfully crude 'being on the rag', or the über-literal Germans with their 'Monatsblutung' (translation – monthly bleeding)? Whatever you call it, there is no denying that our periods get a pretty bad press and 'having Aunt Flo(w) to visit' (whoever thought that one up must have hated their Aunt Flo[8]) is a real pain in the (front) bottom!

But hang on a sec. Are periods really all that bad? Should we, as some scientists and old-school feminists argue, dispense with them altogether?[9] Au contraire! I'd suggest we shouldn't throw in the (sanitary) towel just yet, and consider instead the many opportunities and excuses our periods proffer! Why, when else we can gorge with guilt-free glee on the king-sized version of our favourite snack, or (contrary to the given advice) get off our (exercise) bikes and curl up on the sofa, pretending to be above soppy TV programmes or romance novels (when you are crying inside. Hard). Or last but not least, let off steam at your partner, friend or colleague with issues you wouldn't usually dare to bring up. They should be most forgiving in a few days time when you gently explain with a flushed cheek, 'it was that time of the

---

8 Possibly she was a pain when she came to visit, outstayed her welcome and promised to come back next month!

9 The argument being that historically we were pregnant most of our lives, had fewer periods, and therefore suffered less from ovarian and cervical cancers.

month'. (The latter is especially successful if you betray what some call 'menstrual etiquette'[10] and lay it on with a trowel, adding, 'yeah and it was a really heavy one'.) Because let's face it, on average, our periods last well into our fifties and until scientists prove that it's healthier to do without them, we may as well make the most of them and use them to our advantage![11]

Suffice to say – to look at the advertising campaigns for sanitary products, you'd think we were already out there having the time of our lives, abseiling from K2, windsurfing and whatnot during the misery of our menses. And not only do the advertisers make our (menstrual) blood boil with this misrepresentation of a woman's mood during her period (in fact, do you ever want to be roller skating down the street in white jeans with an inane grin plastered on your face?), the manufacturers and our governments are bleeding us dry with the high prices and taxes we have to pay for them, as if these very basic necessities were luxury goods. Unfortunately, the makers of such 'intimate' products go even further to take advantage of us, playing on our strange insecurities that our periods are smelly and embarrassing. You only have to browse any supermarket shelf to come across the expensive new ranges of scented liners and towels, or discreetly packaged tampons to see that this is true.[12] Worse still are the 'feminine' deodorants available for any time of the month – call me daft but I'd rather smell a little musky or even, God forbid, 'fishy' than exude the 'fresh, piney' scent that normally wafts about in the back of a taxi! Anyway, I'd wager that in most cases, regular washing does just fine … so I'd suggest saving your cash for something a bit more fun and entirely less ridiculous, my menstruating maidens.

10 Indeed Karen Houppert loved the subject so much, she's written an entire book on the subject, *The Curse: Confronting the Last Taboo, Menstruation* (Farrar, Straus and Giroux, 2000)

11 See more on this in Chapter Nine, 'Beats Workin'.

12 Quite who these are aimed at is a mystery to me – grown women surely don't give a tinker's toot, and teenage girls must realise that teenage boys will catch the TV commercials advertising these over-priced 'personal products'.

Contraception

As if periods weren't trying enough, with their arrival we simultaneously have our first sexual awakenings and are perhaps faced for the first time with which contraceptive device to use. [13] Your mother may answer this for you as she frogmarches you to the doctor's office to demand the Pill, or perhaps you and your first love, fair boiling over with sexual excitement, will burn rubber to get hold of those much-needed condoms. As we get older, though, contraception becomes ever more complex and the variety of choice on offer can be pretty daunting – the days are definitely over when we thought the emancipated thing to do was to unquestioningly shove the Pill down our necks simply because it was available. So, ever eager to be of service, the family planning kind in this case, here is the Modern Maiden's quiz designed to help you take control of the array of birth control choices! Go forth and don't multiply, ye maidens!

Question One

Your reaction, if you discovered you were pregnant, would be:

a Thrilled, enraptured and any other superlative you can think of.

b Happy enough, though it could have happened at a better time – perhaps when I'd saved up for it or had a steady boyfriend.

c Pretty pissed off. I enjoy my single life to the full and am careful to look after myself.

d Devastated. Why do you think I am taking a quiz advising me on the most effective form of contraception?

---

13 Well, some of us; others are still playing with spinning tops, rather playing than spin the bottle, when their periods arrive.

Question Two

Your attitude to one-night stands is:

a They suck and I don't … strangers, that is. I like to get to know someone before we get to swapping saliva and other body fluids.

b I've had a couple of one-night stands and felt pretty sorry for myself afterward. I don't think I'll be going down that road again.

c I believe in serial monogamy – but I'm not fussed if the relationship lasts a year, a month or even one night as long as I'm into him … and he's into me (in more ways than one).

d Bring 'em on! I am on a mission to sleep with more men than there were candles on my last birthday cake (and I'm 38).

Question Three

You know the following information about your boyfriend/partner/husband's sexual history (ignore this one if you're a freewheelin' singleton):

a We are childhood sweethearts and we took each other's virginity over the course of a romantic, candlelit … not quite evening; it was more of a candlelit afternoon tea after double maths.

b He's had a couple of serious girlfriends, one of whom has since joined a convent.

c He claims he's only slept with five women but if that's the case, I do wonder how he built up that repertoire in the bedroom!

d He was once a tour rep for Club 18–30. Say no more.

Question Four

Have you ever had an STD or unwanted pregnancy?

a Now you really are sticking your nose where it's not wanted. What do you take me for?

b No. I am always careful to use adequate protection for both my sexual health and contraceptive needs.

c I regret to say, I did have an abortion when I was younger but with the morning after pill readily available these days, I don't see that happening again.

d I've been up the clap clinic more times than a Z-list celebrity. False alarms. Mostly.

Mostly As

You're a clean livin' cookie and no mistake, and if the cap fits, wear it! The cap could be a great solution for you as you sound like you can plan (with five minutes grace anyway) sex in advance, and having had no STDs or previous pregnancies, you only run a smaller increased risk of ectopic pregnancy.[14] A coil is a similar device that is worn at all times and is fitted by your doctor, so you don't have to fiddle around before you get down to it. With your contraceptive device, that is.

Mostly Bs

You seem pretty steady with one main current squeeze, but if you've recently met and your sex life is still a hot bed – room, bathroom or even kitchen table – of activity it could make sense to be on the pill or have the pill injection/implants if you want to avoid a pregnancy so early on in your relationship (having each had the all clear for venereal diseases, natch).

Mostly Cs

You might want to get your partner du jour or du heure to slip on a condom so you don't slip up and end up on a slippery slope to an STD! You should keep a supply of condoms at all times (sounds like you'll need 'em) and see Chapter Thirteen for a handy hint to get one on if he's not 'up' to the job.

---

14 Where pregnancy occurs outside of the womb, usually in the fallopian tube – if using the cap or coil and you fall pregnant, you are more likely to have an ectopic pregnancy than if you use another contraceptive method.

Mostly Ds

Oh you are a one! And while we're on the subject, if you are going to play the numbers game, you really ought to look after number one before your number's up! A combination of pill to prevent pregnancy and condoms to prevent disease are suggested. Nay, implored!

As you should have come to expect, the quiz was tongue-in-cheek (and every other nook and cranny that comes to mind), but if you look hard enough, or even simply read the darned questions and answers, there's a safe sex message in there, too. The naked truth is (but do please put your pants back on if you are currently affected) that although most of us labour under the misapprehension that we'll never catch anything, sexually transmitted diseases are more widespread in the western world than the common cold. So, while I'm all for taking liberties as well as the usual precautions, and for your being a sexual adventuress with threesomes, foursomes and evenmoresomes, let's take a moment to consider why the safe sex message simply ain't getting across.

One of the problems is that many STDs lay dormant, so we can easily catch them from (or pass them on to) every Tommy Todger, Dick and Harry Hard-On we meet, before any of obvious symptoms are on show (puss, warts, crabs and scabs, to name but a fearsome few). Another is that, contrary to what people may think (or hope), much like the butt of a stand-up comic's jokes, age, class, religion and your gender are no barrier to STDs. So, to you older, supposedly wiser, readers, don't think I'm trying to teach grandma to suck eggs, because reports show that the recent increase in syphilis is due to the current fashion for middle-aged 'swinging' parties. (We'll have a gander at these not quite oldest swingers in town in another chapter!)

Despite knowing that STDs are as easy to pick up as a bachelor at a wedding, if you do catch one of these nasty surprises, the chances are you will feel mortally embarrassed and not wish to fess up to your 'little problem'. However, you must run like the clappers to the clap – or to be more accurate, sexual health – clinic, my manky-minkied ones, for the sooner you deal with it, the sooner you'll get treatment and can put your ordeal behind you. And if you are worried about your reputation staying intact, even though your cherry clearly isn't, you can even use a pseudonym when visiting the clinic (this is perfectly allowed; you'd be surprised how many Minnie Mouses they see each day in these places) and inform everyone you've slept with recently.[15]

Even if you are not doing your own version of the 'Itchy and Scratchy Show' just yet, it may make sense to have the occasional once-over, particularly when you meet a new partner. I know this means that on top of our usual cervical smears (which we should have done about every three years) and breast checks, we seem to be on our backs throughout our adult lives as much as for pain as for pleasure, but just grit your teeth and bare your bottoms, ladies! Smears are a very effective way to catch the early signs of cervical cancer and you can't say fairer than that, can you?[16] As for your breasts, mammograms are widely available for the over fifties,[17] but while they can be an effective way to catch early signs of breast cancer, there is a question over whether this painful procedure also involves some element of risk (a debate which rages among health professionals and some feminists alike). If you are under fifty, we all know we should be examining our breasts for unusual lumps and bumps, but what should you look for, exactly? It is worth asking your nurse or doctor if you are unsure, and maybe asking your boyfriend to do the checking – he may be more likely than you to know how your boobs normally feel!

Yes, indeed, the female anatomy brings with it its fair share of womanly woes, not least if you discover you're pregnant … and it wasn't planned. Yep, sometimes our contraceptives fail, sometimes we forget

---

15 This includes telling people who you've used a condom and/ or had oral sex with; condoms are no barrier to pubic lice, and gonorrhoea and syphilis can both be caught through oral sex.

16 One trick to get through this endurance test is to make fists and shove them under your buttocks in order to tilt up for better access. May not be ladylike but does the job!

17 In the UK, Australia and some parts of the US there are free public screening programmes for women aged fifty-plus.

to take or use them, and sometimes we just plain don't bother. We're only human, after all. One way of not letting things get this far is to use the morning after pill if a condom splits or you got too carried away to use one. Then, your first port of call will probably be the pharmacy, as in most western countries, including the UK, Australia and the USA, the morning after pill is now available without a doctor's prescription. This pill is effective for up to 72 hours after you've had sex, with decreasing effectiveness within this time frame. If you're grilled by the pharmacist as to why you want it, simply tell them, 'None of your business!' and make sure they fill you in on the side-effects (particularly if you are on any other medication at the time).

Unfortunately, even the morning after pill can fail, and because of that, or because for one reason or another you haven't taken it, the worst may come to the worst, and you have an unwanted pregnancy. At this point you may consider a termination. In the English-speaking Western world, terminations are legal and available to women who request one in the first trimester of pregnancy, after various hoops have been jumped through, as well as possibly having to deal with right-to-lifers jumping up and down outside any clinic you visit, campaigning to get this legal situation changed.[18] Of course not everybody agrees with termination in principle, but let's just deal for now with the prickly moment when you make your mind up to have one, as tackling such an emotionally charged debate could fill the entire pages of this book.

Whether you take the decision lightly or even decide to go ahead against your principles, you will need your friends and family around you for emotional support. If you have to wait a while for your hospital appointment, the usual pregnancy symptoms could kick in, such as morning sickness and breast tenderness (covered in more detail in the next chapter). This is a bit like being presented with a gift of a lovely pair of shoes … and then being told you can't wear them, i.e. the symp-

---

18 Such right-to-lifers considering the right to the life of the unborn child, no matter what situation the child may be born into, and not considering at all the right of the pregnant woman, to follow the path in life they choose.

toms will be a nasty reminder of what you can't have for financial or emotional reasons (or both), right now. But you must try not to despair. The most modern of maidens will make a decision that's right for them at the time. That's not to say that you may regret not staying pregnant in later life, but you should remember counselling is available, whether at the time of the termination, or several years down the line, so don't be afraid to seek professional help, no matter when you may feel you need it.

And let's not forget that there are those of us whose preoccupation is not how to avoid getting pregnant, but quite the opposite. The next chapter has all the info you need as you launch into this next stage of your sex life (copious amounts of sex to conceive, very little sex afterwards). But you should not expect, just because you are expecting, that you're going to be treated with 'kid' gloves. On the contrary, the gloves are most definitely off! You have been warned!

Modern Dilemma

Dear Modern Maiden,

I know it's not physically possible, but I'd swear my boyfriend suffers from a male version of PMT every couple of weeks. He skulks around the place, lying on the sofa playing computer games, and glugging back lager with almost alcoholic enthusiasm. If I ask him if there's something on this mind, he becomes very defensive and tells me to butt out. Could it be that the much talked-about excess of oestrogen in the water supply is making our blokes as hormonal as we gals?

Best wishes,

Bronnie

Dear Bronnie,

I'm no doctor, but I would diagnose your boyfriend is suffering from his 'beeriod'. Symptoms for this modern male affliction include sulking like a big girl's blouse and grunting monosyllabically in response to questions (inane or otherwise)/attempts at conversation/being asked to switch off the football after four hours of continuous viewing. You may want to closely monitor when his symptoms are most profuse and you might not be surprised to find it's a day or so after a big night out. Hence the definition 'beeriod', otherwise known as 'having had a few too many and being too macho to fess up to a hangover or comedown'. Of course scientists would argue that men do have hormonal ups and downs, just like us, but please don't feel too sorry for him. Until he's bleeding out his willy once a month with gut-wrenching stomach cramps and the temper of a harpy, I'd put his moods down to being a sulky git!

Yours scatalogically,

MM

CHAPTER FOUR

Pregnancy and Birth: Living with Your Bump and Beyond

PREGNANCY

Whether the conception was timed with military precision using an ovulation predictor kit, followed by a cartwheel while the sperm swam for dear life, or it was a 'happy accident', the result of years of umming and aahing (or more accurately, ooohing and aaahing), employing the withdrawal method with your long-term love, or last but not least, down to the briefest of encounters with your man of the moment (okay, of five minutes) in the loos at the local night spot – congratulations, you are pregnant! Or else you are reading this chapter with the sort of sick fascination of someone watching a TV hospital drama – you know there will be tears, blood and guts along the way, but you hope for a happy ending.

Assuming you are going ahead, your first preoccupation will no doubt be when to spill the beans now he's spilled his seed.[19] The given advice is usually to wait until the first three months are up before telling anyone but your nearest and dearest (who, of course, may not be one and the same!). This may be difficult for those who embrace their impending motherhood with hyperbolical hysteria, rushing out to buy an 'I Love My Bump' or 'Baby-On-board' t-shirt. If this is you, I bid you kindly put this book down, look in the mirror (checking out your usual sartorial high standards), and ask yourself simply 'Why?' As far as work is concerned, there will come a point when you will have to tell your employer you are pregnant (varying from country to country, so do bone up on this when you find out the happy news) but it may be in

---

19   Apologies to the squeamish among you but if being this graphic makes you wince, you should question the sanity of putting yourself through the next nine months and beyond of gore galore.

your favour to reveal all asap if you are feeling tired, moody or emotional and want the guys at the office to know why. (An unusual note of caution and solemnity from your author here: the reason many people err on the side of keeping shtum is because of the high incidence of miscarriage in early pregnancy. There, I've done my dutiful bit …)

TRIMESTER DIGESTER

Duty over, and back to that merry moment for many, or indeed most, of you when the little stick you've peed on turns blue and you are beside yourself with happiness at the prospect of being a mum. Enjoy the chocolate-box moment while you can, my with-child chums, because during the next nine months you will be poked, prodded and patronised as never before. Your body will become public property as random strangers feel your baby bump, imparting their wisdom on what sex you are carrying, or that the name Fred, Gordon or Abdul would be an apt one for your future bundle of joy. And that's not even to begin to mention how your life – as well as your backside – will be transformed as the little blighter rears its ugly, and ouch, oh-so-big head.

Don't worry, though, because it's possible to relax and enjoy your pregnancy (I said it's *possible*; I'm not making any promises), and as ever the Modern Maiden is here to help. In actual fact, your first pregnancy can be a useful experience in ways you may never have dreamt of: giving up a job you hate – even if temporarily; allowing you to 'eat for two'; encouraging you to abstain from the grog and fags for a few months, when even the world's finest course of hypnotherapy failed.

You will soon discover that your pregnancy is split into three trimesters (yup, brain box, that's three months per trimester), each one bringing with it a new ailment (erm, I mean, a new cause for celebration). Or, as the old saying goes: three months dreary, three months cheery, three months weary. Well, one out of three can't be bad, surely!

First trimester – Dreary

You may not even know you are pregnant for much of this trimester and, in fact, may have unwittingly been knocking back Singapore Slings with your usual zeal. Don't spontaneously combust with guilt; most doctors will scoff if you tell them you are worried, and in France, it's recommended to drink at least a bottle of Bordeaux every day to keep the baby happy. Okay, slight exaggeration here, but not to put too fine a point on it, unless you've been raving it up each and every weekend there's probably little to worry about.[20] All in all, it's quite usual not to notice any symptoms for the first six weeks, which is lucky when you consider the following.

The Plus Points

⚘ You are pregnant and this may bring you and the father (assuming he's part of the deal) unequivocal joy.

⚘ Er, that's it.

The Downside

⚘ After the first six weeks, for the first time in your life you will be more conscious of your boobs than the most mammary-obsessed man in your life has ever been. A tenderness that would make Otis Redding himself flinch will transform your bosoms into instruments of torture at even the slightest touch. Look on the bright side! This does mean those pesky pregnancy hormones are kicking in.

⚘ It is fairly inevitable that you will suffer from the least aptly named thing in the English language: morning sickness. Who on earth named this 'morning sickness'? 'Morning, noon and night sickness' is an infinitely more accurate nomenclature for this – peculiar to pregnancy – affliction. To add insult to injury, you may not even be sick, merely suffer from tidal waves of nausea when anything less

---

20 Having said that, my qualifications on the science bits are somewhat shady (i.e. non-existent) so best get yourself checked out by a medical professional if you have any concerns.

bland than a bowl of gruel is put in front of you. (Although you may worry about putting the right nutrients the bump's way, you only need seek help when you are throwing up most meals.) I've got a reassuring science bit for you here: ginger is supposed to help, as well as eating little and often. So, if you're suffering from morning sickness (not everybody does) and you'd planned to trough an entire black forest gateau in one sitting as you're 'eating for two', think on!

❁ Last but not least, the three pregnancy dwarves 'Frumpy, Grumpy and Lumpy' will no doubt come knocking at your door: Frumpy – the summer clothes you'd been pining after will be replaced with a desperate search through maternity-wear catalogues for anything sassier than a pair of 'adjustable' dungarees; Grumpy – you will have a veritable fairground of feelings in these early days: mood swings, a roller-coaster of emotions and more frights when you look in the mirror than during a ride on the ghost train; Lumpy – your 'normal' clothes will start to feel a little tight and nobody will give up their seat on the bus for you. At this stage most women look portly, not pregnant. Roll on the second trimester!

Second trimester – Cheery

For most people the second trimester is to be embraced with – if a slightly clumsier grasp than usual – open arms. You could be 'blooming', showing lots of energy and be revelling in the attention from your loved ones that a first pregnancy brings. Enjoy it now, my maternal maidens, because as soon as the little darling shows its face you will become invisible to your friends and relatives as they push past you in the hospital to cop a look and have a cuddle with the crinkly urchin in your arms (despite the stitches, the bandages and the drip hanging out of your hand). Back to the most cheery of the trimesters though, and with your first scan out of the way, and the baby kicking, the least worrying as well. Do try to make the most of it …

The Pros

❀ Mother Nature sure was playing her joker when she made some women feel their sexiest when 'in the family way'. Even if this does not apply to you, it can be fun trying out new positions (before your tummy gets too big), giving new meaning to the phrase, 'bump and grind'! Although do be prepared for the fact that not everybody will feel this heightened sensitivity, and men in particular can be put off sex at this time. If this applies to your man and you are feeling friskier than a customs officer at Amsterdam airport, you might want to gently remind him that sleep won't be the only thing he'll be deprived of when the baby comes along. That should soon get his pecker up.

❀ You may feel energised and should take the chance for some gentle exercise, which should also help you get your figure back[21] quicker after the birth. Such activity should reflect any exercise you were doing before you fell pregnant. If you were a lazy bint beforehand, for example, it's not a bright idea to undertake frenetic aerobic activity and if you were previously a jolly gym goer, there's no reason to stop now. Pilates, yoga and aqua aerobics are all good exercise techniques that can help prepare for the birth.

The Cons

❀ During this trimester, even though you may feel physically well, emotional issues could come to the fore, especially if you're planning to raise the baby alone. Now would be a good time to join an antenatal group to talk with other expectant mums about your worries. Don't expect the bonhomie to last after the birth, though. High levels of oestrogen will probably make your post-birth mothers' meetings more competitive than the dads' race at school sports day.

---

21 If anybody knows where your figure actually goes to before you 'get it back', could they please enlighten me? I imagine a giant waiting room with a load of headless pre-pregnant bodies impatiently waiting to be reunited with their owners!

Third trimester – Weary

You're into the home stretch (marks) now and home will indeed be where the heart is as you become increasingly anti-social and get the nesting instinct. This might find you on your hands and knees in a pair of Marigolds cleaning the kitchen floor repeatedly (even if the closest you've come to being a scrubber in the past is when you rebounded like a rubber ball from your first true love). Relaxation is the key and you must insist on your partner, or friends, pampering you with lots of massages, gifts and healthy meals. Milk it for all it's worth, for pretty soon the baby will be doing the same to you. Literally!

The Upside

❀ You can finally leave work after pretending to be busy for the past month (little did they know your look of concentration was an excruciating decision over the pink, blue or yellow baby-gro).

The Many Difficulties

❀ So many new afflictions to tell you about, so little time.[22] From piles, to nosebleeds, to the comeback of morning sickness, you may feel worse than at any other point in the pregnancy. At a time when you need rest the most, sleep will prove elusive as you toss and turn in discomfort and suffer from weirdly vivid dreams.

❀ The hospital bag is packed, the first teeny-tiny outfit chosen and drooled over with maternal mawkishness, the cradle assembled and ready to rock. But your mini-adventurer is showing no signs of being brave enough to make its final descent into the big wide world. The fact is, many first babies are late. Sometimes very late. Sadly some of the advice given to get things going is misleading, dangerous or just plain wrong! Such as:

---

22 Erm, actually time is one thing you will have at this stage, so perhaps you might like to take up a new hobby: knitting, crocheting or something useful like writing letters to leading politicians about the crap maternity services in your area?

SEX: Most books wittily proffer the advice that even if sex is not a sure-fire way of starting labour, you'll have fun trying! Yeah, nice one! If you think your partner scaling your body as if it were an assault course at this point in the pregnancy is fun, remind me not to come to any of your parties!

CURRY: Another load of baloney (or should that be biryani)? Many people may think curries bring on labour as they have a similar effect on the bowels. Oh, what the heck, let's not be euphemistic: they both give you the shits. Sadly there is no truth in this old wives' tale, and all you will be doing is risking the chance of a dose of food poisoning from the local curry house. If you do go down this route, best to make one at home (and I mean get your partner or a friend to, natch, because you should be sitting with your feet up).

LAXATIVES: As above but less enjoyable as you won't even get a tasty tandoori treat out of your endeavours.

RASPBERRY LEAF TEA/ACUPUNCTURE: If you are feeling hippy-dippy you could try either of these methods. The former acts as a stimulant on the uterus so be sure not to drink it before the last two months of pregnancy. The latter may be recommended by your midwife near your due date but is clearly not for those who are squeamish about needles (an attitude which may swiftly change when it comes to the epidural). More to the point, raspberry leaf tea doesn't appear to do anything, and it tastes gross.

EXERCISE/ KEEPING UPRIGHT. Well, you can't change the laws of physics, and gravity must play some sort of role on the little darling making its arrival. As for exercise, a walk in the park may be, erm, a walk in the park for some of you, but for others a short turn around the bonsai in your living room will be just about all you can manage!

To be honest, you won't be able to wriggle out of a boring, anxious wait until the darling infant is good and ready to wriggle out of you. This may be two weeks late, this may be two days early, but do be reassured that, as sure as eggs is eggs, and as sure as his sperm plus your egg (with luck) have developed into the eager beaver bounding down your birth canal, your baby will come out eventually. So do try to relax until the big moment finally happens. You'll certainly know about it when it does.

Birth

Unlike the event itself, I will keep this section mercifully brief. Principally as I am not a medical professional (I repeat!), and with only one child under my (non-chastity) belt, I am no expert either, the advice in this chapter is therefore purely anecdotal and should be taken with a pinch of salt, or if you are already in labour, with a truckload of gas and air, massage, or screaming blue murder [23] – whatever gets you through it.

The birth itself happens one of three ways in these days of modern maternity: a natural birth – where you go through labour and birth without any pain-relieving drugs or medical assistance; an assisted birth – where you need drugs, intervention – whatever it takes to get that baby out; or a caesarean section, planned or otherwise. This third option has become known as being 'too posh to push' – although I'd wager that if you think having your womb cut open, being sewn up and wearing a colostomy bag for two days is 'posh', then you're beyond help.

Whichever option you choose, is foisted on you, or happens at the last minute, your midwife or antenatal teacher has probably suggested you write a birth plan to give the midwife and doctor an idea of which of the above options you would prefer. This is all well and good, but everybody knows the best laid plans of mice and men – and in this case, mothers – inevitably go tits up. In a moment we can have a gander at a birth plan and the actual birth that followed, but before we do, let's take a brief aside to set out, in laywoman's terms, some of the factors you should include.

LOCATION: Where you plan to have the baby, i.e. home, hospital, birthing centre. And do bear in mind it could be in one of the locations

23 And if you are in labour, shouldn't you have found all this out some time ago?!

of urban myth: back of taxi, supermarket car park, although I appreciate these won't be your first choice.

BIRTH PARTNER: Recent research shows that two-thirds of midwives no longer believe men should be part of the birth since they make poor birth partners and can find the experience traumatic. Diddums! If they make poor birthing partners it's because they have not boned up on their facts beforehand. Besides, nobody should have your best interests at heart more than the father of your child. (Makes you wonder if the midwives don't like someone around who can stick up for you!)

An alternative or addition for those who can afford it is a doula, an experienced woman who offers practical support, before, during and after childbirth. A surrogate midwife, if you will, but one who gets paid in cold, hard cash (by you and not the hospital).

PAIN RELIEF: Two hundred years of medical science and an **epidural** (an injection of a small amount of anaesthesia in the spine) is the best they can do to help mothers through the pain of childbirth. Fair enough; you won't feel any pain but neither will you feel any sensation at all in the bottom half of your body, leaving you totally immobile. This immobility often slows down the birth and commonly leads to further intervention. Thanks, chaps in medical science: it may be 'unnatural' to give birth with pain relief, but so is a seventy-year-old man with an hour-long stiffy, and somebody managed to invent something to sort that out, eh? A recent development is the **mobile epidural**, an improvement on the above as the injection localises the anaesthetic and some women have mobility in their legs. At the time of writing this is available in few hospitals, and generally only private ones (in the UK at least).

The alternatives are **Entonox** or gas and air. The safest, least controversial pain relief, best taken as the contractions build up for maximum effect. Go easy, though, as it's not called laughing gas for nothing, and you don't want to be howling like a hyena when you need to be cool as a cat. **Pethidine** is another drug on offer. A hallucinogenic substance, it can knock you out completely, which is great if you want to sleep through the birth of your child, or hallucinate you are giving birth to a piglet, but not so great if you want to remember the experience of childbirth, however painful.

INTERVENTIONS: Intervention can happen during an assisted birth if the baby is having trouble coming out without help. The following are the more common forms of intervention: **forceps** or **ventouse**, both of which are used to help the baby be born if you are having trouble pushing.[24] **Forceps** are like giant cooking tongs that are attached to the baby's head to help pull it out. A **ventouse** is a less drastic proposition, and is a small cup attached to a vacuum pump which pretty much does the same job.

EPISIOTOMY: An incision made in your perineum which helps if you are having trouble pushing the baby out. Do make sure you ask for pain relief at this stage if you didn't have any earlier on … afterward you will need to be sewn up which is also true if you tear of your own accord.

DELIVERY POSITION: Gone are the days (thankfully) when women were tied to beds to give birth. In your antenatal classes you'll learn about the different positions you can choose, from lying on your side if you are tired of pushing, to squatting if you're feeling energetic, to all fours. Yeah, pretty much think of a sex position and you can have your baby in it.

Now that we've established the facts, let's review a sample birth plan and then reveal the truth about what really happened on the labour ward.

24 Or if the labour ward is full and they need to get you out quickly …

Birth Plan	Actual Birth
Location At home for the first stage of labour, with cosy cushions and soft candle-light, listening to relaxing sounds of gently lapping waves on CD, perhaps using the TENS machine we hired. My partner will drive me to hospital just in time for the second stage where I would like to give birth in the **birth pool**.	**Location (s)** Two hours into the first stage, the contractions came every two minutes. Raced to the hospital on my own in a taxi (partner nowhere to be found) only to be told to go back home as I was only 1cm dilated. Stayed at home for the next 24 hours trying to remember to breathe. The birth pool was available- but had no water in it …
Birth Partner My boyfriend, Nick. He has a child from his marriage before we met, so his hands-on experience will come in very useful.	**Birth Partner** The baby came two weeks early and Nick was in a noisy pub watching the FA Cup Final and 'didn't hear' his mobile phone. My elderly neighbour who does not speak English sat with me, as I attempted to show him how to stick on the pads of my TENS machine – at which point he fled. On my return from my first visit to the hospital, Nick was asleep on the sofa with beer breath and an empty kebab wrapper in his lap. He attended the rest of the birth.

Pain Relief

As a calm and spiritual person, I know I will make do with the breathing techniques I have been practising. If the worst comes to the worst I would prefer **gas and air** rather than any other **pain relief**.

Pain Relief

On arrival at the hospital a second time the midwife said I still wasn't ready for the labour ward, and when I kicked up a fuss she said I might like a shot of **pethidine**. In the end made do with gas and air and reached such highs I asked the doctor, 'Don't I know you from down the Zap Club?', our local nite spot.

Interventions

I want to give birth to my baby naturally with as little intervention as possible.

Interventions

The junior doctor told me to push too soon and I tore extremely badly. Had to have an **episiotomy** and ended up with more stitches than the Bayeux Tapestry.

Delivery Position

Anywhere but on my back.

Delivery Position

Much like the baby's conception, ended up on my back, after all.

The lesson to be learnt here, my labouring lovelies, is by all means write your birth plan, but don't take it too much to heart, as getting away with the birth you dreamt of can often be down to Lady Luck. There's no need to beat yourself up if you end up with an assisted birth (there's always a next time!), and if you do have a natural birth, don't wear it like a badge of honour. You might not feel unbearable amounts of pain in labour, but you will when someone pokes you in the eye as you harp on about the awful women who need intervention. Okay, you may argue that cave women didn't need intervention when they gave birth, but they didn't have running water, beds and doctors, and their life expectancy was thirty. So get off your high horse and get high from that Entonox!

The immediate aftermath

So, by hook or by crook (mind you, let's hope the implements used were slightly less archaic), your efforts have borne 'fruit' and you have welcomed the apple of your eye to the world. But horrible though it is to contemplate, the hard work is far from over, for when (that last agonising) push comes to shove, the real fun starts and a lifetime of motherhood begins.

Before we attempt to cover this minefield of a topic, let's briefly do battle with the first obstacle you'll need to overcome once the birth and afterbirth are over: getting both you and the baby out of the hospital in one piece. If you thought the pre-match build-up was a nightmare, the next hours, days, or even weeks, that you spend on the hospital ward after the birth will have all the drama, anguish, sweat and tears of an especially good football game. Of course, you could be one of the lucky ones and be discharged within hours. If, for whatever reason, you have to stay in hospital (you had a C-section, for example, or if you or the baby have complications), your first request should be for a private room. Not, you understand, because of all the newborns on the ward living up to their reputation and boo-hoo-hooing from dusk 'til dawn, but because their new mothers may also be, well, crying like babies, and if this was not enough to keep you sleep-deprived, there is the constant relay of obnoxious relatives (maybe even your own) and medical staff creating a rumpus as they come and go. Finally, just as you've dropped off after a mind-boggling 72 hours without sleep, comes the deafening rattle of the tea trolley and a gentle shaking of your shoulder,

'Cup of anything, love?' AAAGH!

It is an atmosphere that does not much help in those supposedly crucial first hours and days when a mother should be 'bonding' with her infant. I say *should* as I'm afraid it's time to pull the plug on this myth of immediate bonding, and – switching our metaphors – to rip to shreds the stereotypical Athena-poster-like image of you and your baby, gazing into one another's eyes, filled with instant mutual love and understanding.[25] Indeed, with all the demands a newborn makes on its mother, some Mums may feel they have spawned the devil's own child. And who could blame them? With the bulging eyes, alarming amounts of sticky black poo, and mountains of curdly vomit, shouldn't we be screaming for an exorcist rather than a midwife? In any case, no need to fear if your heart does not melt right away, for much like a romance that blossoms over time, you need to get to know one another properly before you fall in love. This can take days, weeks or longer – even perhaps when they finally give you a minute's peace and leave home in eighteen years time!

In the meantime, back to the hospital room (don't worry, we'll get you out of there soon) where, once upon a time, you stayed on the maternity ward for a week and learned the basics: putting on a nappy; how to breastfeed; how to bathe your baby. Nowadays, that fairytale's over (although I am not sure what our own mothers would have to say about this) and with bed shortages and time constraints, help will usually only come when you have become the woman you so desperately

25 In fact, at this point your baby can't even seen further than the end of its nose, so for her / him at least it ain't going to be love at first sight!

wanted to avoid on the ward: sobbing uncontrollably into your pillow with a cartoon-like cloud of doom hanging over your head. At this point a bosomy midwife may take pity on you and attempt to explain the skill of 'latching on', otherwise known as finding the optimum position for a successful breastfeed. (As opposed to an unsuccessful breastfeed, which feels like someone has taken a pointy, hot knitting needle to your nipple.) Although you may only be producing colostrum, the precursor to actual breast milk, it's worth giving the breastfeeding a try at this stage, as when real milk comes in latching on becomes a whole lot harder – as do your boobs! Yes, soon enough, your breasts will fill up to the size and texture of a pair of rugby balls, with gargantuan nipples looking like a couple of gorilla's thumbs, making it very tricky for your baby's tiny rosebud mouth to suckle. You may also become part of the 'jet set', squirting and shooting surplus milk in each and every direction every time your baby cries.[26]

One trick, if you do have an excess of milk, is to express into a bottle with a manual or electric breast bump,[27] in order to avoid painfully engorged boobs. However, it's a vicious circle and this may mean you end up producing more than an over-subsidised French dairy farmer! Another, less exhausting way to mop up the excess is (I kid you not) to put cold cabbage leaves in your bra for twenty minutes. Nobody seems to have bothered to research why this works, but trust me (and thousands of other grateful mums), it does! And remember to remove the soggy leaves carefully, as, like Bon Jovi, they're Slippery When Wet, and you don't want to be doing yourself or your partner an injury if they end up strewn all over the floor. As if the indignity of engorged mammaries wasn't enough! And while we are on the subject of indignity, let's not forget that for the next five to six weeks you will suffer from lochia, the post-natal bleeding (the breaking up of the lining of the womb) that unlike menstrual bleeding (see previous chapter) can

---

26 Or indeed at any baby's cry or image – like a friend of mine who left her baby at home to have lunch with some other mummy friends and was soon leaking all over the place as they swapped baby pictures!

27 This is also a really good idea in order to get the father or any other eager helper to give the baby one or two bottle feeds a day and let you have a bit of a breather or your first 'proper' night out for nine months!

smell like the backdoor of kebab house in high summer, and is more copious than the very worst period you ever had. Welcome to the joys of early motherhood!

Mother knows best?

You'd be mistaken in thinking that once you finally get the baby home from the hospital (See? I told you we'd get you out of there eventually) life will be a bed of roses (indeed, more like a bed of poo, leaky milk and cabbage leaves for the next few weeks!). For, where the old adage 'mother knows best' might have once rung true, a more suitable modern maxim would be 'mother knows worst', particularly if she is variously a teenage mum (all she wants is a 'free' flat and benefits), single mum (sponging off her ex-partner and the State), working mum (a selfish bitch whose children will be monsters), or lately, sexagenarian mum[28] (while women are unnatural and weird giving birth over the age of 59, men who father children at this age are super youthful studs). Yes, now that you have joined the ranks of motherhood, you can bid a frenzied farewell (everything you now do will be at double speed) to the old you, a person in your own right, and will be judged from the moment you give birth 'til your dying day on whether you are this year's model of a 'good mum'. And don't think for a maternal minute that simply because you've done your bit for society by sprogging that your every (career) move won't be under the microscope, or that your every word and action as a mum won't be inspected, and that your every maternal choice disrespected by all and sundry (and by all I mean from your mother-in-law to the bloke in the corner shop where you buy your nappies).

It doesn't help when women themselves can't agree on what constitutes successful motherhood. Recent books and newspaper articles com-

---

28 For clarity's sake, we mean here mothers in their sixties, not mothers having sex, which is probably just as rare!

pound this, talking about the 'mommy wars'[29] of stay-at-home and working mothers fighting it out over which choice is the best for their children. Such running around in circles stops us from asking another equally valid question: what is right for us (or do we relinquish all our human rights as soon as we become a mum)? Even as we disagree on this we are busy causing one another grief, judging other new mums on our post-pregnancy looks. Sadly, it's no longer acceptable to look 'mumsy', the dictionary definition of which is 'homely and unfashionable'. Yes, we can but reminisce about the times when we could float round the house in a colourful kaftan or Laura Ashley dress, gracefully covering all our (natural) lumps and bumps. Now the prevailing look to aspire to is the 'yummy mummy', the totally half-baked idea of looking as if you never gave birth at all! For these women have perky boobs as opposed to whopping melons, taut tums, not post-pregnancy paunches, and are more well-groomed than well-grimed in baby debris![30] And even though we know these washboard stomachs sure as hell aren't simply down to twelve weeks of breastfeeding, we feel inadequate when her next door is back in skin-tight jeans only three months after giving birth.

Right then ladies, in view of this mummy madness, it's clearly time for a wake-up call (although I am well aware that most of you are in no need of an alarm clock)! What's say we ditch the bitchiness, dump our attitude to frumpiness, and make peace with our motherhood and each other? Let's unite and invent a new, sassier approach to motherhood, no longer 'mumsy' or 'yummy mummies' but let's instead be 'yumsy', that is, let's acknowledge that nobody's version of being a mother is the right one and just do what's right for us. Let's recognise that there are more things that unite us in motherhood than divide us; and finally, let's decide to accept all the changes that motherhood brings (stretch marks, flab and all) without losing sight of our old identities.

---

29 The latest being the imaginatively titled 'The Mommy Wars' by Leslie Morgan Steine (Random House, 2006)

30 In fact, when pushing the buggy, they'd be glad to be mistaken for the au pair.

Mother's little helpers

In order to convince you that we can all be 'yumsy' and we have more in common than you think, here are a few hints and tricks to get through the maelstrom that is the first few months of motherhood (which should be oddly familiar to most of you existing mums out there).

❀ If you have the baby blues, don't spend all your time with other new mums. Whereas before the birth it was fun to gossip with your pre-natal group, after the baby's born there will be more oestrogen running through these meetings than an entire country's water supply. This can make conversation competitive, and sometimes even downright nasty. Things can get especially bad when someone asks in a smug tone, 'Have any of you done it yet?' A valid question in some ways, as your first sexual encounter post-birth is as much of a rite of passage as losing your virginity (and can be just as painful). However, if you are already struggling with new mother-hood, you don't want pressure from your mates on this front as well as from your husband/partner. Clearly you should do it at the time that's right for you (for instance, if you had an episiotomy, you will have to wait for the stitches to heal) and otherwise, keep it zipped! (Or unzipped, the point is, it's up to you!)

❀ You may find yourself driven near crazy by the lack of freedom the new baby brings and find yourself wishing your life away, gazing enviously at the retired couple at the table next to you in a café. In fact, never mind retirement, you will probably fantasise about having a day, nay an hour, or even five minutes to yourself in the near future. If your partner or co-parent is less than understanding about this need for solitude, simply paint yourself a 'do not disturb' sign and as soon as he gets home from work, run like the wind and lock yourself in the bathroom for as long as it takes to unwind (you may need to take in supplies as this could take a while!). During which time, as he cares for the baby alone, it may dawn on him that you too have done a full days' work, and then some, by the time he comes home.

- No doubt the prevailing emotion in your life will now be guilt: for example, for having a wee when baby was crying for a feed; for poring over parenting books when the laundry needs doing; or for ignoring the phone when you know it's your own mum ringing up for a chat (to be fair she's probably feeling guilty about you!)[31] Whatever. I suggest fewer Hail Marys and more bloody Marys – or whatever else your poison is – because, let's face it, you couldn't feel any more guilty than you already do, so you may as well indulge in a guilty pleasure while you are about it.

- Hanging out in the evening with friends without kids will help you get off that one-track mummy mind. For you'll find, especially in the early days, that socialising with other parents makes the conversation, almost involuntarily, swing around to the topic of kids. Better to hang out on occasion with childless friends who will help you claw back some of your old identity. They may want to hear about you (not the baby) ... or you may even completely push the boat out and want to talk about them and their lives.

- Dress to suppress! Yes, instead of driving yourself mad, worrying about not fitting yourself into pre-pregnancy clothes, buy some new clothes in a larger size and forget about those lumps and bumps for now. You have more important things to worry about! And remember: pattern prints are good, not only to disguise any lingering curves but to hide the inevitable vomit stains.

- Accept every offer of help you are given, even if it's from the batty old dear at No. 5 who wants to do your washing up, or if your favourite aunty offers to drive for over two hours just to bring you a home-made casserole. Any time you can get to yourself to gather strength is worth it. And even if you are feeling on top of things, who wants to do their own bloody washing up anyway and well ... aunty's cooking always was your favourite!

---

31 Yes, guilty about the stupidest things, when you are clearly doing the very best you can.

Never mind. If being a new mum is both the best and worst thing that ever happens to us, perhaps we can take comfort in the fact that our efforts will be recognised and 'rewarded' once a year on Mothering Sunday. A day when, if you're very lucky, you can look forward to breakfast in bed and a lie in and if you're very unlucky you will be given *The Hits of Johnny Mathis* or the *Soppiest, Most Loveliest Romance Songs Ever* on CD. This will seem strange if you've had a life-long love of banging techno or thrash metal, but then, we only have to look at the marketing campaigns surrounding this annual event to see that mothers are perceived as one giant homogenous mumsy lump. And the fact of the matter is, my sentimental sweeties, even if you do receive such an utterly inappropriate gift, you will treasure it. Since whatever our kids do, we love them anyway. And that, I suppose, is one of the things us mums can all agree on (phew, found one in the nick of time just as the chapter ends!).

If the above hints and tips are not enough to see you through the next eighteen years, maybe the next couple of chapters will help. But perhaps you're not ready to turn to drink and drugs just yet! In this case, remember 'yumsy' not 'mumsy' and give a boot up the bum to a yummy mum!

Modern Dilemma

Dear Modern Maiden,

I recently gave birth to my first child and have spent the last few weeks mastering the art of breastfeeding. I'm worried about making the next step and nursing my baby in public, as friends tell me total strangers have confronted them for doing so – I'm shy and don't want to cause anyone offence, but after all my hard work, I don't want to have to make do with the bottle and formula milk when I'm outdoors.

Yours sincerely,

Lily

Dear Lactating Lily,

Sorry to say it, but we ladies sure got the booby prize when it comes to attitudes to our anatomy. Happy to steal a glance at the tits on the top shelf of a newsagent, or see them wiggled in their face at a lap-dancing establishment, men can be awfully sniffy about seeing breasts used for their actual physiological purpose. In surveys you see about such matters, it is mainly men who say that while women should have the right to nurse their babies in public, there should be segregated, designated spaces to do so (missing the point that when baby is crying for his/her supper, there is nothing that can be done other than to wop your breasts out there and then). But don't be discouraged: if you have a good nursing bra, and a comfy baggy top, there is very little on show, so try not to worry on that front. And I'm sure that, if anybody did get sniffy, you'd have another three people stick up for you in this day and age!

Yours encouragingly,

MM

Dear Modern Maiden,

A year ago I gave birth to a lovely baby boy, my first child. Sadly, instead of feeling blissfully happy as I anticipated, I have a permanent feeling of disappointment, and that I am missing out on life away from my family commitments. I gave up an exciting job to look after my son full-time as my husband earns more than enough to look after all of us. I can't help feeling resentful about what I have given up and am missing my old life terribly. I dare not mention this to any of my friends, who either seem happy to stay at home and look after their kids or can't afford not to work. From the outside looking in, we have a perfect life, so why do I feel so bloody miserable?

Best wishes,

Rosie

Dear Rosie,

There are some who would tell you to pull yourself together, to be thankful for what you have, and suggest that you are merely the type to think the grass is greener (remember those long hours you put in at work, for instance, or the boss and colleagues who drove you nuts). However, I think you are probably suffering from the disappointment that dare not speak its name. Simply put, for some, looking after young children, even if we love them deeply, can be boring in the extreme. From a practical point of view, you should discuss your feelings openly with your husband; you never know, maybe he yearns to stay at home with the babe or would be happy to go part-time so you could work a half-week as well? That you have a permanent feeling of disappointment worries me, though, and it could be that these feelings run deeper than the usual baby blues, so maybe it's time you sought professional help. Chatting to someone outside your circle may offer a breath of fresh air, and will help you get a sense of perspective on things.

Yours maternally,

MM

CHAPTER FIVE
From Beer to Eternity

Booze has had a bad press recently: a bucketful of vomit-soaked images have saturated our TV screens and newspapers, with reports of a nation so getting into the spirit of things that we are drinking more vodka per capita than the Russians.[32] At this stage I'd like to point out that what you are actually seeing is the same image regurgitated a zillion times across the different media (the image of some poor lass who's teetotal, and throwing up a dodgy curry in the street.) All of this garlanded with a sensational cocktail of headlines, bemoaning the rise of the 'binge-drinking culture' in our cities, towns, shires, villages, hamlets, cardboard boxes and so on.

But I am here to tell you this, my boozing buddies: The culture of intoxication – drinking for the sole purpose of getting drunk – goes back as far as the Vikings (and you wouldn't argue with a Viking, would you?). What's more, the generation pissing and moaning about our alleged over-indulgence hammered back the Cinzano Bianco with reckless abandon before we were even born – and in many cases, about half an hour before we were conceived as well. Think, too, of our grandparents – a sherry in the morning, a beer over lunch, at six o'clock the cocktail hour followed by a cheeky gin and tonic.

The very term 'binge-drinking' has been twisted and is now over-used; the term originally meant drinking over a prolonged period, perhaps days, until you could drink no more. Now, I know some of us have free time and spare cash on our hands, but there is shopping to do, our favourite trashy magazine to read, a billion TV channels to tune into,

32 Okay, I made that but up but who knows how close we are to catching up?

so frankly, who can afford (in any sense) to be pouring liquor down one's neck for days on end?

It seems us girlies are the ones bearing the brunt of the moaning minnies' cries for moderation. We're told we've taken over from men as the nation's number one lushes, swilling Chardonnay down our gullets with more gusto than at a piss-up in the proverbial. Well, about time too, I say! Too long we have been the ones tied to the kitchen sink, wiping up snotty kids' noses while our other halves had all the fun propping up the bar down the local. Now it's our turn, ladies, and I'd like you to take your new responsibilities seriously; I'd like you to prove that women, as well as men, can go on a harmless bender without causing a heated debate.

As such, in this chapter you will find a plan for the ultimate binge-drinking session, a dusk 'til dawn low-down on where to drink, what to drink and when to pass out. A handy flow chart will measure your progress throughout the evening to ensure you imbibe the maximum units of alcohol possible. Then, lest you thought I was irresponsible, we will look at the result of your endeavours, your hangover, and grade and deal with it, according to its level of severity.

How to achieve the ultimate binge-drinking session

6pm. Begin by choosing the hostelry nearest your place of work so you don't miss out on a moment's valuable drinking time. Order a large glass of the cheapest white wine available, and get chatting to your annoying workmate whose tedious office politics are guaranteed to get you quaffing at a super speedy rate.

The Modern Maiden's top tip: Don't overeat at this point in the evening or you will be soaking up well-earned units too early on. A light snack of salted peanuts should be enough to line your stomach.

The measure of your progress:
1 large glass wine = 2 units

8pm. You should by now be on your merry way to tiddlyville. It makes sense to hang out with your work colleagues a little longer as they are more likely to shout you drinks than your tightwad mates. If they don't, drag them to the nearest chain bar, which is sure to have the best

The measure of your progress:
2 more glasses of wine= 6 units

happy hour or two-for-one drinks promotions. Remember though, shameless yet blameless: Wear a hat and/or sunglasses if you must drink in such an inferior establishment.

Nice one! You are already officially binge drinking according to the UK Government's figures.

10pm. Having managed to ditch the saddos from the office, you should now move on to more elegant surroundings with your real friends, having tanked up on cheap lighter fuel earlier on. You should treat yourself to a sophisticated cocktail (whilst you can still read the menu), in a venue playing uplifting sounds. Be warned though: with this much petrol in your tank you could transmogrify into Ms Nasty Drunk rather than Miss Blissfully Tipsy, so think bellissima, not belligerent!

The Modern Maiden's top tip: Now might be the time for a tactical puke – rather do it now in the privacy of a water closet than in the gutter in front of your mates later on. For the virgin vomiter, the trick is to put your fingers down the back of the throat and wiggle.

The measure of your progress:
1 cocktail = 8 total units

12pm. The latest top nightspot beckons. Try to avoid over-exuberance with the bouncers or you won't get very far. On entering the premises a couple of vodka shots wouldn't go amiss to get the party started.

The measure of your progress:
2 vodka shots = 10 total units

The Modern Maiden's Top Tip: Another warning! Prowling men just love to come onto a girl in an intoxicated state. Make sure you discard your beer goggles for some (se)x-ray specs, to sift out the lovers from the losers.

2am. Is that the glitter ball on the dance floor spinning, or is it you? Either way, the evening would not be complete without a novelty drink. A Flaming Sambucca normally does the trick and has added danger value!

The measure of your progress:
2 Flaming Sambucas = 12 total units

The Modern Maiden's top tip: Three is definitely not a crowd as you make your way home. Licensed cabs are always a good idea. Let your author remind you – it's all about having fun … but getting away with it in the morning.[33]

4am. That home-brewed peach schnapps that has been festering at the back of the cupboard for a year will now seem mighty appealing. Swig back a shot's worth (no need for the dignity of a glass at this point) and ride the rough boat *Quease* to the land of Nod.

The measure of your progress:
1 peach schnapps = 13 total units

The Modern Maiden's top tip: Take two aspirin and drink a token glass of water for your head's sake tomorrow, and place a bucket by the bed for easy access, just in case.

---

33 Especially as – and without wishing to rain on your party parade – alcohol has become the new 'short skirt' when it comes to rape, namely, that women can be accused of having 'asked for it' if drunk when attacked (whether by a stranger or not). Not that this should stop you drinking, or indeed going home with someone for sex – but do think twice about whether they'd really be that attractive or nice-seeming if you hadn't downed fifteen pints.

You've surpassed yourself, consuming in just one night the total maximum number of units women are meant to drink in a given week!

Well done. You have now completed a lesson in getting rip-roaring, ankle-twisting, pants-wetting, moose-snogging, stomach-retching, kebab-eating drunk! Go forth and liquefy, my sisters!

The morning after the night before

This morning ain't going to be pretty, and you may need to take it one toe at a time, as you try to rise with phoenix-like resolve from your stinking pit. Never one to shirk my duties, especially since I may have led you into this sorry state of affairs in the first place, please allow me to now offer various hangover 'cures' according to the level of your difficulty making it out of bed and into work.

Level One

You awake feeling suspiciously chipper and get up with a smug spring in your step, rather proud of how 'hard' you are when it comes to hard drinking. Unfortunately the moment you get to work and try to do anything more strenuous than surfing the web, waves of nausea and tiredness hit you and you seek an instant fix.

The Cure: Many of us would find this fix in the form of sugar or caffeine but, believe it or not, a healthy approach might also be a good way to rid yourself of this minor hangover (and it is minor, my malingering maidens, so pull yourselves together!). Eating a banana will replace potassium lost to alcohol's diuretic effect (when you are pissed – you pee). And if you can manage it, a little exercise will help those naughty toxins sweat out of your body quicker.

Level Two

Your mouth is gacky and dry, and your stomach whirls like the spin cycle on your washing machine. You have a slight throb in your head from dehydration and it is getting worse by the minute.

The Cure: Shove a can of fizzy pop, two Ibuprofen capsules and a salty snack down your gullet as soon as you can with all the bravado you were showing last night. The peeing problem means you won't only lose potassium but salts from your poor overworked body, and it's the lack of these that is making your head pound and stomach churn. Your body also needs sugar to break down alcohol and you therefore have a valid excuse to indulge in a full-fat can of cola for once!

Level Three

You wake up after two hours sleep, stumble bravely towards the shower and attempt to brush your teeth to get rid of the liquor and vomit fumes steaming out of you in a miasmic stench. Sadly, brushing your teeth only makes you retch further, and there's nothing for it but to stay in the shower until you've spilled your guts (while trying hard to miss your feet).

The Cure: 'The hair of the dog that bit you'. That is, get a slug of booze down your neck sharpish to delay the agony. The science behind this one is too complex for a laywoman like me, but trust me, it works.[34] It is, however, only a temporary, ahem, measure, and you will be putting off the inevitable hangover 'til later … at which point proceed to level four.

Level Four

Just like you mixed your drinks last night, you now have a toxic mixture of each of the hangovers described above. Quite simply, you wish you were dead (or are contemplating murdering the 'friend' who cajoled you into 'just one more', or the idiot who suggested tequila – oh – yes – you remember now, it was you!).

The Cure: There ain't none. What do you expect? I'm not a miracle worker! All you can do is lie in the recovery position and repeat to

34 Oh alright then, booze contains ethanol and methanol, the latter being the really nasty poison which will make you feel like caca. Because the liver deals with ethanol first, if you down more booze, you are delaying the agony of it processing the ethanol. Tada! Hangover postponed. I learned this at: http://www.bbc.co.uk/dna/h2g2/alabaster/A103140 so, again, trust me, I didn't make it up!

yourself in a lullaby voice, 'never again, never again' in the hope it will soothe you into a sleep from which you will never awake (or at least 'til the thirteen lovingly imbibed units from your binge-drinking sesh are out of your system). Let's be honest though, there always will be an 'again' – but do yourself a favour, and give your liver a chance to recover before you do it any more damage.

As much as I'm all for the excesses of a good night out, it pays to reward your over-taxed liver (and the rest of your booze-addled bod) with a bit of a detox now and again. Hit the carrot juice and super-food-salad as soon as you're over the hangover hump, and you'll be making more than a token effort at warding off the longer-term alcohol-related nasties like liver damage and even cancer … but you're big enough and ugly enough to work that out for yourselves aren't you, my little hung-over harlots? And if alcohol isn't your poison and you're into something a little stronger, then read on, as the next chapter may be the, ahem, fix you need!

Modern Dilemma

Dear Modern Maiden,

Every time my (usually sweet-natured) best friend consumes the demon drink, she becomes unbearable, spoiling for fights and basically ruining our nights out. I am the one who bears the brunt of her ill humour and bad behaviour but if I mention it to her the next day she claims she can't remember a thing, becoming nothing but sweetness and light again. I am not sure how much longer I can take it … Can you help?

Yours desperately,

Florence

Dear Fed-up Florence,

My old boss used to say, 'Don't play the hero in the evening, if you can't play the hero in the morning.' But it sounds like your friend is definitely the villain rather than the hero of the piece! You don't say whether she's a big drinker apart from on your nights out, but that's no matter – it's sometimes not how much we drink, but our relationship with alcohol that can be the problem. And, like all relationships, it's often our friends who notice when things are going tits – or in this case bottoms – up, before we do. It may sound cruel, but recording her behaviour on a camera phone or, better still, video, may shame her into accepting she has a problem. And if she sees red rather than seeing sense, you may have to walk away from your friendship for a time to see her think, if not act, soberly.

Yours hopefully,

MM

Dear Modern Maiden,

In January I resolved to drink much less than last year, giving myself at least a couple a days a week off the sauce. I am finding this extremely tough as I have to attend a lot of social functions in the evening (which invariably involve alcohol) because of my job. At the moment I am drinking a bottle of wine at least four nights a week. I am too embarrassed to seek professional help, but would be interested to hear your thoughts. Do you think I'm an alcoholic?

Yours truly,

Emma

Dear Emma,

At least four bottles a week? Gulp! Or shouldn't that be, 'don't gulp!' since you are trying to cut back? I guess you don't need me to tell me that this is way beyond what constitutes sensible drinking (yes, there is such a thing). Unless your job description states 'must drink far too much to see her through events' and you're being paid by the glass, the work excuse simply won't wash. If you must attend these functions, try alternating drinks, soft and boozy (pick something with bubbles and nobody will spot the difference or indeed care). Possibly, like many of us, you are dependent on alcohol for a boost when tired or feeling nervous, but I'm not in position to diagnose whether you're an alcoholic! If you're too scared of going to the doctor, there are tests you can do on-line which can help you to try and answer this question. Or, you could do something drastic and change careers … perhaps teaching or long-distance lorry driving. Anything that keeps you indoors or in transit, and out of the pub and liquor cabinet, has got to be a step forward!

Yours abstemiously,

MM

CHAPTER SIX
Something for the Weekend?

When it comes to the drugs debate nowadays, public figures fall into two camps – the 'haves' and the 'have-nots'. Inhaled, that is. Of course, the former are in the minority and tend to be rock and roll stars or high- (high indeed) profile bad boys and girls, while the latter encompasses anyone with an ounce of social responsibility (not that kind of ounce, gal pals, so put that doobie down and concentrate!). Since I've no intention of starting a career in politics and don't have the looks or talent to become a celebrity,[35] and despite the fact that I'm not the kind to spliff and tell, I thought it would be in the reader's interests if I came boil-wash clean about my own cannabis inhalation technique. However, allow me to leave you on tenterhooks for just a moment while we blast back into the past to consider times when the drugs issue wasn't … well, simply wasn't such … an issue.

Let's begin in the nineteenth century, when opium dens were as ubiquitous as Starbucks and nobody batted an eyelid, the long arm of the law included. (To be fair, batting an eyelid must've been tough when everyone was skagged up to the eyeballs.) The current Establishment might want to remember that Queen Victoria herself, whose very name conjures up thoughts of abstemiousness, liked the odd toot of snuff (she was, in fact, at times very amused indeed). It wasn't until the 1920s that opiates became harder to come by, and had to be bought on prescription (in the UK at least, with the 1920 Dangerous Drugs Act).

If we go back even further, to the reign of Elizabeth I, anyone owning

---

35 Whoops. I forgot! Talent or looks are irrelevant in the celebrity world these days. Perhaps I should not be so hasty.

over seventy hectares of land was required by law to grow hemp.[36] Roll on four hundred years to 'LIZ II – The Return', and if you're found growing even a single cannabis plant you'll be strung up quicker than saying 'Pass the dutchie on the left-hand side, Your Majesty.' Yes, today in our 'prim-issive' society (permissive, my arse) drugs are yet another social taboo, and the scale of their use[37] is swept under the carpet (much like all your drugs paraphernalia when the fuzz come knocking at the door).

This brings me back to the question of my own drug use and inhalation method: yes, I've smoked cannabis and, yes, I inhaled, but, erm, just not very well. (Give me points for trying, but I'm asthmatic and was once told by a doctor I've 'the lung capacity of a monkey'.) But yes, I'm one of the millions – probably including some of you – who use or have used drugs 'recreationally'. This basically means using drugs for leisure or pleasure, perhaps only occasionally and (in most cases) without becoming an addict.

Yet fessing up to this hedonistic hobby remains fairly unwise. Despite the violence and related crime that surround the drug trade, and despite research into drug use by the UK government (which showed that ecstasy and LSD are 'less harmful' – both physically and to society – than tobacco and alcohol), the taboos surrounding these drugs dictate that they should remain illegal.[38] So, do yourself a favour, and if you are going to partake of 'dirty rugs', don't do a Kate Moss and get caught. What's more, my tempted temptresses, remember that drugs make you lose your inhibitions, and can make you act, well, like a bit of an idiot. In which case, it's best not to try them for the first time (or indeed do them at all) at the annual family barbecue, or on a first date.

---

36 Not for personal use, you understand, rather it was used to make cloth and rope for the ships to defeat the Spanish Armada.

37 800,000 ecstasy users in the UK alone. Source: *The Independent*, Tuesday 1 August 2006

38 Source: *The Independent*, Tuesday 1 August 2006, as above. Yes, although ecstasy in particular was eighteenth on this list, in terms of the relative harm of legal and illegal drugs, the UK government have chosen so far to ignore the advice of their own Senior Ministers to reclassify it as a Class C drug. Alcohol, on the other hand, came fifth on this list, which might provide more food – or rather, drink – for thought in light of the previous chapter.

For other tips if you are thinking of trying drugs, or are worried about someone who has (or indeed if you just want a 'trip' down memory lane), here is the Modern Maiden's brazen yet blameless guide to the more popular 'recreational drugs' to be found on our streets, in our nightclubs and up our nostrils every Saturday night.

LSD

Aka: Acid; Trips; Tabs

Definition: A hallucinogenic drug, that will either have you weeing yourself with laughter or crying for your mummy for twelve hours solid.

The basic facts: Trips come in a small square piece of paper that you put on your tongue (usually with a 'groovy' design which can help identify how strong a trip they're going to be, a microdot being the strongest and possibly best avoided for the novice user). They take twenty minutes to two hours to start working, so don't double drop because the world hasn't turned topsy-turvy just yet. The effect can last for twelve hours so don't make plans to have Sunday lunch with your granny the day after you've taken it (unless she is an ageing hippy, in which case, why not take it with her?).

The highs

- You might laugh uncontrollably at anything and everything. As the world goes wibbily-wobbily your senses will work overtime – walls can start moving, plants talking, and so on – all of which can seem hugely amusing.
- There may be an increased sense of connection with your friends, and you might find yourself saying or thinking the same things simultaneously.
- You might, on the other hand, retreat into yourself, and start pondering *life, the universe and it*. Just don't be fooled into thinking your deep philosophical insights will survive the trip back to normality.

The Lows

- A bad trip is worse than bad. You may go through your own personal journey of paranoia, anxiety and fear.
- You may have flashbacks of bad trips at entirely inconvenient moments, up to several months later, e.g. at your granny's funeral, walking down the aisle, etc.

The MM's advice on acid: It's best not to take a trip if you're not feeling tip-top or have a tendency toward paranoia; this drug will only exacerbate these negative frames of mind. If possible, avoid sex on acid, especially if one or other sexual partner is straight (in the sense of sobriety). It can be terribly off-putting to the straight partner if the tripper ends up screaming with laughter or in fear, rather than crying out with shouts of lust.

Speed

Aka: Billy; whizz.

Definition: An industrial-strength stimulant that will give you bags of energy.

The basic facts: Comes in a powder form and is snorted, dabbed on gums or swallowed. It looks much like a household cleaning powder – and much of the time probably is, as speed tends to be cut with other things to keep the price down. All physical activities and tasks will take about a nanosecond to complete. Take care, though, as it will do strange things to your intellect, so don't undertake important work or essay-writing under the influence or you could end up writing more repetitive gibberish than you'll find in a political party's manifesto. It won't take long to work and it lasts for hours.

The Highs

- If you like to party hardy, speed will keep you going from dusk 'til dawn and then some.

- You won't feel remotely ashamed about your new dance moves, even if they involve gyrating on a pole pretending to be a snake (your straight boyfriend, on the other hand, might not find this snake-charming, erm, charming).
- Cheap as chips (although infinitely less sophisticated).

The Lows

- You may feel higher than Mount Fuji when you are on it, but the comedown is worse than having your feet run over a cheese-grater while hot knitting needles are poked in your eyes: just imagine that bittersweet, empty, post-coital feeling and multiply it by the biggest number you can think of (which on a speed comedown will be no higher than four).
- The conversation may be flowing like wine at Roman orgy, but do try not to talk at people, or give them your life story if you've only known them for five minutes, that is, if you want to know them for five minutes more.
- Remember those pictures of the old fellas who took part in gurning contests? Well, they will look prettier than you, because speed makes you grind your teeth and pull the stupidest faces. Long-term use can and will change your pearly whites into stumpy brown pegs.

The MM's speedy suggestions: If you must take this filthy drug, put it in a cigarette paper to make a 'bomb' and swallow it, otherwise pus-filled yellow crustaceans will inevitably appear on your throat in a couple of days. Chew gum to stop your teeth rotting and – with any luck – stop you being such a loquacious loser.

Cocaine

Aka: Coke; Charlie; Charles; Sniff.

Definition: Another stimulant that provides an instant hit, it will have you feeling Queen of the World – well, for the thirty minutes or so that it lasts – and won't you just want everyone to know about this cocaine coronation!

The basic facts: An expensive powder, usually snorted through a rolled-up note, this is not the drug of choice for penny-pinchers with only a little loose change in their pockets. The 'hit' lasts about thirty minutes and leaves you wanting more.

The Highs

✹ The shyest wallflower should get a confidence boost from the white knight.

✹ You could spend a night in the world's most boring city (my nomination: Stuttgart) and think you'd hoovered up your way to party central.

✹ Coke can make you feel energetic and alive, chatty, and as if you've hit the big time.

The Lows

✹ This drug is more-ish beyond belief (particularly if you've taken it in the form of crack): think of your desire for a bumper bar of chocolate after you've been on the cabbage soup diet and times it by a squillion. Not only can this make the drug habit-forming, it can also turn your cash flow into more of a trickle.

✹ You may think you're Lady Muck, with your highfalutin tootin' habit and will want to share it with the world, but your mates and acquaintances may think you've just become a self-centred bore.

The MM's cocaine counselling: I think the following story of urban myth shows how low we can sink if we've become dependent on coke: Girl walks into a bar where she chats to sleazy guy, who on hearing of her need for a line of the white stuff, offers her a toot if she goes down on him in the lavatories; said girl performs the dastardly deed. The chap zips up, straightens himself, says, 'You might want to think about what you've just done.' And that, my dears, is the moral of the story on coke.

Cannabis

Aka: Weed; puff; blow; hash; The 'Erb (hippies only); ganja.

Definition. The only natural (unrefined) drug from the fair cornucopia of intoxicants we are discussing here.

The basic facts: Cannabis can come in bud form (weed, skunk) or as a resin (hash) and is usually smoked in a variety of ways. It can also be eaten, chocolate brownies being the usual serving suggestion. Regular users tend mostly to be manboys (they can't quite decide which), who have smelly bedrooms with Bob Marley posters on the walls way beyond their student years.

The Highs

* Just one toke of skunk and you could be laughing your socks off. Your favourite comedy programmes could become even more side-splittingly funny (and even serious news programmes might have you guffawing the night away).
* Your appreciation of art, music and film might be enhanced. Particularly anything by Bob Marley, Pink Floyd or the Beatles' White Album.
* Regular users find it relaxes them and that it gives them a deeper insight into the ways of the world.

The Lows

* You may become so relaxed that you end up slouched on the sofa, wearing blimb-burned jogging bottoms, while eating a mega-stuffed crust pizza ... every night of your life. Not good for your waistline, your social life or indeed your bank balance.
* Can trigger psychological problems, and long-term use can be habit forming.
* If smoked with tobacco, can obviously do all the things tobacco does to you. Like, erm, kill you. Better to use a pipe or chillum and smoke it in its purest form, in this case.

The MM's thoughts on pot: Things beginning with b are not for the first time user or for the faint-hearted, so avoid bongs (water pipes), buckets (home-made bongs) or brownies if you don't want to throw a whitie (this is when the world starts spinning, you have a dire need to vomit and your skin turns a whiter shade of pale).

Ecstasy

Aka: E; Eccies; Pills; MDA; MDMA, disco biscuits.

Definition: A stimulant originally conceived as an appetite suppressant for soldiers in World War One. Later rediscovered and used as a drug to help with marriage guidance counselling and even later rediscovered (again) as the clubber's drug of choice.

The basic facts: Mainly comes as a pill or capsule, but MDMA (the purest form of ecstasy) and MDA are sold as a powder in wraps. Comeup time varies from twenty minutes to an hour and is signalled by a tingly feeling in the hands, or other body parts. If you are taking ecstasy for the first time, you may need to vomit or poo. Depending on the quality and what it's been cut with, it lasts four to eight hours.

The Highs

❀ One drug that does what it says on the tin. You should feel ecstatic, euphoric and exhilarated, and should be able to dance for hours on end.

❀ They don't call it 'loved up' for no good reason. Your worst enemy could become your best chum and you will want to stroke and fondle everyone and everything, inanimate objects included (chairs, pillars in nightclubs and lampposts will not escape your E'd up clutches!).

The Lows

❀ You can easily become dehydrated on E, so remember to take on board about a pint of water every hour if you are partying hard and take time to 'chill out'. Not too much water, though, especially if you are not sweating profusely.

● Unfortunately, you will become indiscriminately amorous, hugging everyone in sight, including that sweaty topless crusty with the soggy and matted chest hair.

The MM's MDMA moments: E can bring on the need to poop, so do take some toilet paper with you to the club or you may end up caught short (or inadvertently using your train ticket home and get stuck on the streets for the night). Orange juice helps bring you down if you're too far gone, and bananas will replace lost potassium if you end up with disco flu days after your 'session'. Bananas can also help with the emotional trauma of your come-down, which can last well into the week after your night out (or in).

THE LOWDOWN ON COMING DOWN

Talking of which, and lest you thought I was irresponsible for doling out advice on taking such strong substances, perhaps it's best if I give you the, ahem, dope on come-downs and other possible ill effects of taking your nasty narcotic. A slight discomfort as you start to come down may be 'Ugly Eye', a scary phenomenon which occurs when you are going home after a night out, only to find everyone else is getting up for work. In your sleep-deprived and drugged-up state, the commuters you are sharing the train or bus home with take on the guise of leering gargoyles, and you may shift about uncomfortably in your seat in a bid not to catch their eye. As your come-down worsens you may get 'The Fear', a feeling of mild paranoia. At this point the commuters *know* what you've been up to, and are chastising you with a simple blink of an eye. 'The Fear' can continue well into the next day after a drugs binge, and may develop into a creeping sense of panic that you did something outrageously stupid or offensive the night before.

Something for the Weekend?

Unfortunately, if you take drugs over a long period of time, this fear can become an everyday reality, verging on paranoia, even when you're not on anything. Clearly this is the point when you should take stock and perhaps take a break from regular drug taking. Paranoia aside, let's not forget the numerous consequences for your physical health if you have taken drugs recreationally over a number of years: the eroding of your nasal passages from too much coke; scattiness and memory loss from any of the aforementioned; or heart problems from taking too many amphetamines or other stimulants. Not that you may not suffer similar consequences, or worse, if you smoke tobacco or drink alcohol, but it'd be a fool who said you can snort your way to party central every weekend without some sort of fallout.

There you have it. We didn't end on a 'high', so this may help you decide that drugs are not for you (or bring back memories of why you stopped doing them). Or, you may throw caution to the wind and find yourself wishing Es rained out of the sky like hailstones. Either way, you should inform yourself about what you're doing and 'Just Say Know!' to drugs.[39]

---

39 I got this witty catchphrase and some of the historical information about drugs from http://www.urban75.com/Drugs/drugreen.html – worth checking out for further information, and for info on other recreational drugs not covered by this chapter.

Modern Dilemma

Dear Modern Maiden

I recently moved to the Big City where I was shocked to see that illegal drugs are everywhere: at upmarket dinner parties; in down-market nightclubs; even in the local market where more than just the potatoes are 'home-grown'. I desperately want to fit in with the new friends I have made but I always have been, and always will be, anti-drugs. How can I convince my new friends I'm cool if I won't partake in their filthy habits?

Yours sincerely,

Candy

Dear Cautious Candy,

Drugs can be fun. Drugs can give you a new perspective on the world. Sure, drugs can help you make new friends. But cool? I'm not sure. Is there really anything cool about relying on a powder or a pill to make a night out fun, or to give you the confidence to speak to people? At the same time, if drugs are prevalent in the circles you move in, your 'anti-drugs' stance may be a little strong. Nobody should consider you uncool if you turn down their offer of a line or a puff (peer-group pressure should definitely be left at the school gates), but they almost certainly will if you start preaching, or try to force them to see the error of their ways. Perhaps you simply need to broaden your horizons, if not your attitude: the city's a big place and I am sure you'll find like-minded folks if you keep looking.

Yours advisedly,

MM

Dear Modern Maiden,

Is it just me, or have drugs become increasingly shit? If it's not me, do you know where I can get hold of any good ones?

Yours,

Dinah

Dear Dinah,

I am afraid I cannot help you on two fronts: firstly, it would be irresponsible of me to point you in the direction of any particular dealer's door in print (I like my face the way it is!), and secondly, even if I could help you out on this score (pun intended), I would have to agree that the quality of illegal drugs seems to be on the decline. Just as we notice the cost of drugs like cocaine and ecstasy going down, so it's also become clear that the quality of these drugs is getting worse (as both are being cut – and cheapened – with ever-more dodgy substances). Cocaine, for example, is being cut with the carcinogenic painkiller phenacetin that has helped its street value drop over the last few years. (Mind you, this drug can also be found in cigarettes, so headlines on this subject only further illustrate that double standards are never far away when the media talk about illegal and legal drugs.) A further, perhaps unwelcome, thought would be whether you've ever considered it's not the drugs that have changed, but you? I'm not suggesting you hang up your raving shoes just yet, but if you've been overdoing it, or have to consume more and more to get the same effect, then having a bit of a break could be just the tonic you need!

Yours party-poopingly,

MM

CHAPTER SEVEN
How to Survive the Nine-to-five

Life's a bitch. For proof of this canine conspiracy, we only need look to history where women have always worked like dogs, have been treated like dogsbodies, and usually work for some greedy, drooling mutt who laps up all the proceeds! Planting rice in the paddy fields of India and Vietnam, suffering the tedium and footache of working the shop-floor in the retail trade, sweating laboriously in Britain's nineteenth-century cotton mills or working in the twenty-first century equivalent, the call centre, are all 'women's jobs', and all have much in common: they are low paid, hard work and, in the main, are usually scorned by men.[40] However, if we took a health check of the status of women in work – in the Western world, at least – we are certainly on the road to recovery, even if we don't get a clean bill of health just yet. Men's jaws no longer drop if it is a female doctor asking them to drop their trousers; a woman walking into a boardroom won't auto-matically be asked to pour the coffee (although she may get a second glance); and with more female world leaders than ever before, we gals are finally getting a go at the tippity toppest jobs on offer.

But feminists would ask us not get too excited at these apparent success stories, so let's pause for thought, my career-minded chums. They would argue that as hard as we may try to earn an equal living, there is still all too often an ethos of 'jobs for the boys',[41] and that in many industries a barrier to our reaching the pinnacle of our chosen careers, to our smashing through the so-called glass ceiling, remains, and that even if we do make it to the top, we are not paid the same as

---

40 Call centre work in the UK is seventy per cent done by women, thirty per cent by men. Source: www.unison.org.uk/acroba

41 Note that even when we talk about nepotism we don't talk about 'jobs for the girls'.

our male counterparts. Some may also suggest that office culture remains a laddish phenomenon, a testosterone-charged beast, where only by locking horns and being bullish (arguably male qualities), can we make the leap from the metaphorical factory floor to the boardroom.

How much of this rings true will depend on your age, race, class, where you live and how you earn a crust. And there's no escaping the fact that some women voluntarily put their careers on hold, or settle for less-challenging roles, when they decide to have children and raise a family. But there is still some way to go until we have total workplace equality, and let's agree that if success at work has long been a man's game, it is time to turn the tables and make it a woman's game instead. If this means redefining what is acceptable to get on in our chosen careers when discrimination holds us back where our skills and talents shouldn't, then so be it.

Sound interesting, my ambitious angels? Sure, you might think, but how do we go about it? We could start by bringing emotion (arguably a female quality) into sterile business dealings, [42] or even going as far as getting our legs over to get a leg up the career ladder. How far you go (in so many ways!) is up to you. But maybe by using our female sassiness and savoi faire we can reverse the machismo culture of office life and infiltrate the 'old boy network'. Maybe, by breaking a few rules and making up a few of our own, we can reverse hundreds of years of an unfair male advantage in the world of work. And just maybe, a new generation of women will be unafraid to use their feminine charms and intuition as a backlash against the laddish environment in many offices across the globe. Desperate times call for desperate measures, after all!

HOW TO SURVIVE THE NINE-TO-FIVE

It was the Queen of Country Music, Dolly Parton, who famously sang

---

42 For example, when trying to sell your company's latest product, don't be afraid to use emotional blackmail, eyelash-batting, or simply boo-hooing, to get your way!

about the monotony and drudge of doing the nine-to-five, summing up the feelings of workers the world over, of the exploitation, boredom and counting down the minutes until the weekend. Having established the precarious position of women in work, let's now have a bit more fun with the following tips for surviving this nine-to-five existence. Let's have a cheeky chew over how to progress our careers with a little shameless, yet blameless, behaviour, and if possible, change the laws of physics and speed up time to get the clock to tick that bit faster toward five p.m. Not that I'm assuming anyone's career is in need of a boost, or that your professionalism is in doubt, my diligent darlings, but perhaps these sassy strategies will help tip the career balance in your favour, rather than tipping you over the edge!

Nine a.m.

A zen-tastic way to start the working day is to come into a clear desk or workstation.[43] Even if your bedroom at home resembles something of a natural disaster area, it is worth de-cluttering your work space to give the impression that your mind is more an oasis of calm, rather than a volcano on the point of eruption. This means removing desk accessories, such as Gonks, trolls or any other hideous plastic creature, the 'I Hate My Job' or similar desk plaque, as well as the numerous pictures of your pet kitty in fancy dress, if you want anyone to take you remotely seriously. If your job involves a mountain of paperwork and you loathe filing, simply stuff your bottom desk drawer with the offending articles. If no one has asked you for copies within three months by all means do file them – in the bin. Thus, you will appear a sea of tranquillity while underneath you a storm of missing papers brews.

---

43   Assuming you have one. If you are lucky enough to work in the great outdoors, I guess you may already be feeling naturally zen. And if you work from home, the opposite applies: unless you have a ready supply of inanimate objects to talk to, you may spend the entire day without speaking to anyone!

Ten a.m.

If your husband/partner/lawyer usually calls at this hour, it is worth asking them to send an email instead. Nobody wants to hear you ranting and raving with your tales of love, squalor and impending divorce, while they try to get on with the business of the day.[44] More to the point, you should try at all times to come across as the office goody-two-shoes if you want a shoo-in to the boss's, um, shoes. (And if you are the boss, you should be leading by example.) Email allows us to exploit our employer's time in a way personal phone calls would never have allowed. However, I'd advise a note of caution here. Some employers spy on their employees' emails, and won't be impressed by your sending three gigabytes' worth of spam to your co-workers (and neither will the recipients, who all received the same ridiculous emails over a year ago).

Eleven a.m.

Around now, as our sugar levels dip and boredom levels rise, sweetness leaves the room and the office banter can kick off. This can sometimes amuse, but can also be downright spiteful, or indeed, hurtful. There is a fine line between sophomoric attempts at comedy and its nasty big brother, bullying. No doubt humour is an essential part of office life, but if you are the only one being singled out for teasing and it makes you uncomfortable, you'd be well advised getting yourself known as a comeback queen. As such, it is always worth getting to know your colleagues' Achilles heels. Then, if the baiting gets too much, a quick witty retort will soon have any bullies off your back and your colleagues on their backs with laughter. Alternatively, if you don't want to come across as a bully yourself, pre-empt the nastiness with a round of tea and a bumper pack of chocolate biscuits. That will soon bring back the sugariness in the air!

44 Or rather, they do, but are you sure you want them to know your pet name for your husband (Big Bobby, for instance), or why you are due to appear in court the following week?

Noon

As things get busy in the pre-lunch frenzy, you might be able to slip in a spot of brown-nosing while your co-workers are too busy to notice. Use your feminine charm and intuition to pick out someone in a position of power or responsibility and ask them to be your mentor, doing so surreptitiously in order to keep the respect of your peers. Most bigwigs will be flattered to be asked (it will make them feel even more important), so choose wisely according to how much your arse licking will get your career ambitions licked. A mentor will prove very useful when it comes to decisions on redundancies or pay rises three months down the line, when you, the boss's secret pet, will be the cat that gets the cream and your less-than-clever colleagues will be sick as dogs! Likewise, it pays to butter up the people who you guess are secretly running the office: the dishy porter, receptionist and post-person. Keeping on friendly terms with these people will definitely open doors for you (in more ways than one where the porter's concerned)!

One p.m.

Your lunch hour should be just that. It's all too easy to grab a sandwich sitting hunched over your desk, or grabbing just five minutes in the staffroom, trying to impress all and sundry with your conscientiousness. This is fine if you do have something urgent to finish, or your job demands more hours than are available, but if you are beavering away just for effect, then give yourself a break (literally). Doing something constructive will be more relaxing and de-stressing than trying to look industrious as you become ever more zombie-like and spaced out from concentrating too hard. A trip to the shops or gym are all well-known lunchtime forms of recreation, but don't rule out visiting a gallery, writing to your grandmother, or, if you're a single gal, checking out online dating websites. Such activities will see you through, happy and relaxed, to five o'clock and beyond. As for lunchtime drinking, this will see you through to five o'clock a little too happy and too relaxed.

So if you are a lunch-hour lush, do make sure you have a strong coffee and a pack of mints to hand, to help you survive the afternoon (assuming you make it back to the office at all).

Two p.m.

If this is the hour of your daily company meeting, it is worth taking five minutes to think about how you can improve your communication skills. An instant way to radiate professionalism is to toilet-train your potty mouth, and use a more grown-up form of communication instead. (Not that f-ing and blinding ever hurt anyone, but if you try to save it for the homestead, you will appear to be keeping your head at headquarters.) Here's a handy trick. Every time you feel like swearing in a meeting, bite your tongue and sublimate your rage with business jargon to come across cool, calm and collected. Replace 'For fuck's sake, you loser, that's the lousiest thing I ever heard,' with 'Maybe you could rethink that paradigm,' and you'll be well on your way.

'Ballpark figure', 'executive decision' and 'blue-sky thinking' are all suitable expressions that would never pass your lips under normal circumstances (and make you sound like a bit of a twat), but they will lend an air of authenticity and gravitas to your negotiations if used selectively, correctly, and, last but not least, sparingly.

Three p.m.

At three o'clock your boredom threshold has probably been well and truly crossed, and your geeky neighbour who was picking his nose and eating it this morning may suddenly take on the guise of a toned Adonis whispering sweet nothings in your ear. Daydream all you like, but remember the rules of office attraction mean that, when suffering from employee ennui, colleagues will radiate between three and eight times more attraction than they truly possess. Which isn't to say that some aren't the genuine article – you are, after all, aren't you? And indeed, many people do meet their beaus at their place of work, so a brief word here on office romances: discretion is pointless. Eyes, mechanical and otherwise, are everywhere, and lack of privacy unavoidable, although a little nookie in the store cupboard is to be applauded (everyone will think you're up to no good anyway, so you may as well make the most of it)! And finally, since we seem to be so prolific at workplace wooing, when starting a new job, you should ascertain who's who in the coupling stakes before bad-mouthing the stuffy old fart with halitosis in marketing, to his dear lady wife of twenty years (or worse, his illicit liaison of fifteen minutes).

Four p.m.

By now you are back to your daydreaming, and having fantasised as much as you can with the available material, your mind may start to wander to other matters, such as how on earth you are going to get out of this hell-hole they call a place of work. If it's truly hellish, and let's maintain the underworld analogy, you might become devil-may-care and start scanning employment websites or the newspaper for new career opportunities. If you are very discreet, you could apply now while you are feeling motivated. Or, you could do the sensible thing and wait until you get home. Either way, let's take a slight detour to think about how you can make the best journey to that coveted new job.

First, let's establish a quick checklist of what your CV and covering letter should and should not contain. Lies, typing errors, coloured paper with cute cartoons or icons, and not tailoring the letter to the job advert are all a little dim. Embellishments (everyone does it), a personal approach, business-like stationery, and attention to detail will make you stand out as a bright spark. Having worked your magic with your application, the next step will be to survive the job interview. It is often suggested to imagine the interviewer naked in order to combat nerves. Poppycock! Indeed, thinking about his cock (if it's a he) could either send you into fits of laughter or shudders of lust. Nerves are to be expected and the person interviewing you (if merciful) will make allowances for this. What they won't expect or make allowances for is bad breath or bad manners. A little effort will go a long way on your road to jobsville!

Five p.m.

Home time – if you are lucky (I am well aware that the nine-to-five is a misnomer in today's hard-working environment) – and time to revert back to the real you, where you can swear to your heart's content, be as rude as you want to everyone, and make more mess (and be happier) than a pig in shit and you won't get the sack. On the other hand, your working and social lives may be intertwined, and socialising with colleagues may be the natural end to your working day. A word of warning here, my loose-tongued lovelies! Not everyone at work will be as friendly as they seem, and indeed there will be back stabbers ready and waiting for you to say the wrong thing at the wrong time, which is usually after your fifth glass of wine!

Speaking of which, let's finish this chapter with the most difficult task you will ever have to face at work: surviving the office Christmas party. To maintain any respect, dignity, status and any other similarly serious sounding synonyms you can think of, in the workplace, the final golden rule for workplace survival and getting ahead in your chosen career is not to attend. Yes, you may sensibly book a taxi for midnight, plan to drink water between each alcoholic beverage and resolve wholeheartedly not to tell Wayne in accounts that you've been lusting after his chunky thighs ever since you sat opposite him in the canteen. The problem, however, is that the minute you hit that flea-ridden restaurant/disco reserved for under eighteens/venue available at the last minute, your willpower will go out the window (along with your inhibitions) quicker than you can say 'free bottle of cheap plonk for each member of staff'. We all know the time-honoured consequences if you don't heed these party-pooping words of warning. But if not, allow me to fess up to my own festive faux pas, so that you may learn from my mistakes of Christmases past. Consider my passing out on the front steps of the boss's home and colleagues being so alarmed they called an ambulance, or taking a dishy colleague back to my flat … a flat shared with my boyfriend of ten years. I've also been caught by my boss *in flagrante* with the spoddiest boy in the office, who just happened to be her son. I don't think I need go on. It's up to you whether you ignore my years of (bad) experience and laugh in the face of party danger, my rowdy revellers. 'Tis the season to be jolly silly after all!

And if you wake up the next day wondering how on earth you are going to face the office, when you can't even face your breakfast, then read on, because in the next chapter we will deal with how you can get away with a well-deserved lie-in (well, the Christmas party would have been boring without you, wouldn't it?) or if you did something controversial and really can't face the music, how to call in sick.

Modern Dilemma

Dear Modern Maiden,

My boss (male) is devastatingly handsome and is a true, old-fashioned gentleman. Or so I thought, until I stayed back late at work last week. He came over to my desk to say good night, and as he leaned over to look at something on my computer, placed a hand on my back and (I'm in no doubt) started fingering my bra strap. I was very flustered and immediately made an excuse to leave, but I am sure he was making a move on me. The thing is, I am in line for a promotion next month and I wonder whether sleeping with him would help or hinder my chances. Advice, please!

Name withheld

Dear working girl,

I am all for flashing a smile, a bit of leg, or even cleavage to further your career (especially if he is a dish), but you need to be sure that going as far as he desires would achieve the desired results. The next time you work late, wait for him to make his move, but don't let him get as far as he wants … when you have him begging like a hungry puppy, bring up the promotion as a joke and see how he reacts. You should only put out once he has signed on the bottom line, if you don't want to be disappointed. On the other hand, you might want to try to gain promotion on your own professional merits, but only you can know if your skills make this a realistic possibility.

Yours collegially,

MM

Dear Modern Maiden,

I work in a testosterone-fuelled environment and have to put up with a fair amount of stick for being the only girl in the office. I don't mind the banter, as I can give as good as I get, but am missing out on important networking as often the post-work social activity involves trips to topless bars or even lap dancing clubs. I am now considering putting my principles – and my spectacles – to one side, as there is a major job coming up I'd love to work on, and the planned schmoozing of the new client involves not only booze, but boobs. Help!

Yours ambitiously,

Sadie

Dear Sadie,

You don't mention which industry you work in, but it could be one of any number prone to such exclusive behaviours, I suppose. No matter. The dreamer in me would like to suggest you ask your male colleagues whether they (or indeed their wives and girlfriends) are really happy about this apparently enforced after-hours activity. They may surprise you with the answer and you could then legitimately suggest another pursuit in order to woo your client. The realist in me imagines the activity is non-negotiable and it really is only a matter of whether you decide to take part. If you do go along, you may just feel like an escort girl, hanging around to add to the general eye-candy, or there is the small chance your colleagues may be shamed by your presence. If you really can't face it, why not suggest an old-fashioned business lunch with the client himself (I assume it is a he) for a bit of gentle one-on-one persuasion. After all, you have assets (the non-financial kind) that your male colleagues will never possess, so use them to your advantage!

Yours traditionally,

MM

CHAPTER EIGHT
Beats Workin'

'Life moves pretty fast. If you don't stop and look around once in a while, you could miss it.' A perfect description of the breakneck speed of modern life. The beliefs, not of a fancy French philosopher in the tradition of Voltaire and Descartes, but of the hilarious high school student Ferris Bueller. Ferris it was, who, in the hit 80's movie *Ferris Bueller's Day Off*, pulls history's most successful sickie.[45] Twenty or so years later, his teenage philosophy stands the test of time. In fact, you could say it rings truer than ever, because the momentum of life in the twenty-first century has accelerated to an almost supersonic degree. Today we want everything in an instant, from breaking news and our evening meals, to our sexual climaxes, and we also – thanks to the wonders of email, the internet and mobile phones – seek immediate answers to the most pressing and most inane questions alike. (Meaning we put about as much thought into 'Will you be home in time for dinne?' to 'Will you marry me?')

If we were feeling hard done by, we could argue that it's we lassies who suffer most from this post-modern pandemonium. Not only do we struggle with our work/life balance more than our men-folk, but we also have to put up with it taking us twice as long as them to do many everyday things: getting a haircut, reaching orgasm, and going to the loo, to name but a few! It's no wonder, then, that research shows women are more likely to take sick days off work than men[46] – we need the extra time simply to get on with day-to-day living!

---

45 If you haven't seen *Ferris Bueller's Day Off*, I can only assume you are very young, very old or very culturally challenged!

46 Source: Benenden Research 2005

I'm not implying we should start playing truant from the workplace at our every whim: clearly good girls win accolades and the hearts and minds of their colleagues, while blatantly bad girls earn nothing but trouble. But then again, nor am I suggesting that we shouldn't take an extra day of rest whenever we need it, or roll into the office an hour or two late from time to time. It's simply that we need to learn how to get away with it à la Ferris. Therefore, in this chapter, we'll take a look at how to handle things if you are running late, how to take a sickie and get off scot-free, and finally, what to do if it all becomes too much and you decide to leave your job for good.

PARTY HARDY MAKES YOU TARDY

The last thing any nine-to-fiver needs is to gain a reputation as the office party girl. Not only will you keep lechers at bay if you personify the virtues of maidenhood in the workplace (even if you party out of hours like a girl from 'da hood') but with the name of office square, you can get up to so much more than your loud-mouthed colleague with the bad rep.

If you've been a DSO[47] after a night at the D.I.S.C.O., it therefore pays to cover your tracks to keep up the pretence of being a wholesome workhorse rather than a lazy lush. Even if you are suffering from a raging hangover, extricate yourself from the alien bed, as well as any sticky situations, and get into the office on time if you possibly can in order to avoid suspicion. A change of clothes kept carefully hidden in your bottom drawer will aid your disguise as a DOW (dowdy office worker) rather than a DSO (as before) for two reasons. Firstly – let's be blunt – you may stink (of what depends on last night's activity). Secondly, and more importantly, the eagle-eyed post boy may notice

---

47 That's Dirty Stop Out to those not in the know. A term generally assigned to young ladies who spend the night away from their own bed ... and in somebody else's!

you are wearing yesterday's garments and will be sure to ask questions. He knows everything, remember? If you wear a uniform to work, so much the better – nobody will notice a thing.

If you wake up late, make sure you have a repertoire of inventive, yet believable, excuses for your tardiness, and call ahead to buy yourself some extra time. In the modern world of a work-shy labour force and mistrustful management, the half-baked, 'My alarm clock didn't go off,' just won't cut the mustard. Why not, for instance, blame your husband, boyfriend or flatmate for locking you in when they left for work or, if you are feeling dramatic (and borderline unethical), say you've had a break-in that has left you all shook up. Whichever excuse you choose, when you do finally show your face, don't bring attention to yourself by babbling a well-rehearsed speech like a bad actor fluffing their lines. A simple, suitably embarrassed, 'Sorry I'm late' will do. The fact you've phoned ahead should be sufficiently crawly.

Mind you, if you plan your big night out well enough in advance, there won't be any need for last-minute excuses. You should save your doctor's or dentist's appointments for the real thing, but there is no limit to the other engagements you can make use of as your one-way ticket to a lie-in.

- ❀ Your bunion, corns or warts need laser treatment. Your boss won't be able to look you in the eye – helpful if you are a bad liar. (Any other non-invasive, icky health procedure will do the same job.)
- ❀ You have to wait in for the rat catcher (your house is overrun with vermin) or plumber (your toilet is blocked by a giant poo) or any other tradesperson to deal with an embarrassing household mishap. Again, the more awkward you come across as you relay your news, the better.

And if you can't be bothered or are too hung over to even make up a story, never mind making the journey in to work, then read on, my lazy lovelies!

MASTERING THE ART OF SICKIE-TAKING

Sometimes our weekends and holidays (and duvet days, if the terms of our job allows for them)[48] simply aren't sufficient to catch up with our day-to-day chores, and we come home from a hard day's work to a laundry bin piled to almost architectural proportions and a kitchen so filthy even the mice have taken refuge elsewhere. At other times, simply winching open a mascara-clogged eye is enough to make us wince, as we ride the rough boat Queasy to the Port of Hangover. These are the times when we may become desperate enough to do the dirty on our bosses and pull a sickie, go AWOL, or whatever else you'd like to call taking a cheeky day off work by feigning illness. For some, to do so is morally reprehensible, criminal almost, cheating your employer out of a day's paid work, and lying to them to boot. For others, the illicit nature of taking leave without permission makes the occasion all the more joyful. Indeed, these folk may reason that, if sickie-pulling were to be criminalised, no judge in their right mind would ever convict.

Let's now delve a little deeper into this criminal comparison, and take a light-hearted look at how you can plan, execute and get away with your illegal day of leisure.

The planning

Like all criminal masterminds you need to plot your wrong-doing in devious detail. To make any feigned illness seem authentic, it is worth clutching your tummy, having a dizzy spell (even pretending to faint if you are a good enough actress) or putting talc on your face to appear wan the day before you go off duty.

---

48 A specific number of days in addition to your annual leave to use if you are feeling tired or run down. Common practice in the US, and with luck, reaching the rest of the world some time soon!

The accomplice

If you have an accomplice, ask them to give you a buzz the day before your fictitious illness, and have a conversation about your oncoming 'symptoms' while your boss or colleagues are in earshot. Your accomplice could also aid and abet when you do the dastardly deed of phoning in sick. Take heed though, as it is best to make this call yourself for maximum credibility, and do please spare your boss the amateur dramatics by speaking in a normal voice, especially if you are not using tonsillitis as your excuse!

The alibi

The most important element for your day of law-breaking leisure is for your employer not to find any evidence, so it pays to concoct a more imaginative alibi than the flu if you don't want to get caught (unless you are ordinarily an exemplary employee, in which case, this is your one-time get-out-of-jail-free card). You could do worse than exploit the workings of the female anatomy (even if your boss is female, but particularly when they are male) to earn extra days off. The more gynaecological your fake symptoms, the more credible your alibi will be. For instance,

'I can't come in today because I've got a really claggy period' will be more believable than an evasive, 'Er, I've got women's problems.'

In fact, since there is no limit to our physical sufferings, let's get our own back by making the most of them to gain as much time off from work as possible. If you're short of ideas, the following timetable for truants may prove useful.

One or two days leave	Bad period pains
Three days grace	You need to have a D and C (when the lining of your womb is cleaned out – a minor operation for major sympathy votes!)
One week of domestic bliss	Bladder or kidney infection
Up to one month's vacation	Pregnancy complications. NB You will probably need a doctor's note for this one. Oh, and a baby at the end of nine months … but you could always borrow one, or leave the job.

If you think it's going too far and a tad anti-feminist (if you are that way inclined) to take advantage of our bodies in this way, why not invent an infestation of an embarrassing and infectious disease, such as nits, threadworm or scabies (particularly believable if you have young children who are prone to such hideous horrors)? Don't underestimate how far these delights will solidify your alibi.

The crime scene

If you plan to be absent for more than a day or two, the crime scene should be prepared lest any snoops decide to pop round offering tea and sympathy. Boxes of tissues, hot menthol drinks, or buckets if you've said it's food poisoning (although please note above for rather more original excuses) should be strewn at will, your bedclothes rumpled, and a dressing gown to hand in case any of your kindly co-workers should pop round to wish you well.

Leaving the scene of crime is not a brilliant idea but if you must, try to keep to your local neighbourhood. If you decide to take in a movie or shop the sales, it's Sod's Law that you'll get spotted by a colleague. The only way you'll escape is if your colleague is also dodging work – result! You've made a friend!

The getaway

Having ensured there is no evidence against you, you have nearly suc-ceeded in getting away with your sickie. Don't blow it now by making a failed re-entry back into civilian life. Putting on a hoarse voice, particu-larly if you've used gynae trouble as your excuse, just won't be convincing. A shy 'I don't want to talk about it' will keep your colleagues guessing and their noses out of your business. And try not to make an accidental slip-up in casual conversation. 'Oh yes, I had lunch with Ruth on Tuesday', will have eyebrows raised and your alibi in tatters.

A final word to the wise

Remember: there is no point feigning illness if you fear you will suffer remorse and come clean to your employer. You will need to be flawless and give in to sin to make it worth the bother! (If you do experience a heavy dose of guilt, you can always make up the time the following week.) And here comes the boring bit: don't forget that if you get caught red-handed it could lead to disciplinary action or worse. What's more, compulsive sickie-taking will not only be frowned upon by your boss, but by the co-workers who have to pick up the slack in your absence, so try not to make a habit of it. You don't need to be a martyr to the cause of office fair play, but a little consideration to your col-leagues will go a long way. Remember, shameless yet blameless, my wicked time-wasters!

ALL WORK AND NO PLAY
MAKES JANE A DULL GIRL

If, sadly, you don't heed these words of warning and err on the side of hedonism, and turn up late and call in sick whenever you fancy, you may end up getting the boot. Or maybe it's you who can't stand the heat and decide to get out of the kitchen, schoolroom, oil rig or wherever else you happen to be employed. Either way, leaving your job can be as delicate a negotiation as the interview to get hired in the first place, and as such, here is the Modern Maiden's method on earning gainful unemployment.

If you resign

1   It is wise to write a polite letter of resignation to your line manager, thanking them for all the help and guidance they have given you in your career. Thus, with luck, you should receive a glowing reference for your next employer. On the other hand, the exit interview with personnel is confidential (or rather, should be) and is where you can go for your boss hammer and tongs if you've got a secret axe to grind.

2   Your leaving party is your parting gift to the company, a little something to remind them of you for the days and weeks to come. It therefore goes without saying that accepting offers of free drinks all evening, drinking the bar dry, then weeing your pants in the gutter at the end of the night will negate your hard work disguising yourself as the personification of professionalism, and you will literally be pissing away any cachet you've earned during your employment!

3   Speaking of parting gifts, the tradition of colleagues having a whip-round, collecting money for a present is a lovely one, granted. However, it makes sense to put in a few hints with a close colleague if there is something you particularly fancy: a golden clock for the

mantelpiece would be nice (perhaps), but that dinky new handbag you were after, even nicer!

4   Nobody will expect you to do any meaningful work during your notice period. So, erm, don't!

If you are asked to leave

1   Do treat your dismissal as if you have been kicked out of a particularly bad nightclub or event. Swagger out of the building in a rock 'n' roll style, head held high, and make it clear that you were too cool for their party anyway.

2   Don't be tempted to wreak havoc and revenge on your employer. Well, if you must, don't do anything incriminating. Dog-do through her letterbox or cyanide in his tea are a wee bit obvious. Starting industry rumours that he wears girl's knickers or she has a penchant for well-hung octogenarians ought to do the trick!

3   Do devise an exit strategy that means you can take all your contacts and important information to your next firm. Therefore, before you swan off, head held high as in point one, take your time to photocopy your contact cards, and make sure to clear your desk, as well as your computer, of all incriminating personal information.

4   Don't mention that you were fired on your next job application. A brief gap on your CV while you did voluntary work at the local donkey sanctuary or 'found yourself' at a Tibetan silent retreat will be easier to explain than why you stole the petty cash or slept with the boss's husband!

Remember what Ferris tells us when he pulls his sick day extravaganza? We need to stop and look around to make it worth the while, so make sure you take the time to stop and smell the roses on your sick day or lie-in, and especially if you have been given the boot. Read a favourite book, rent a classic DVD, or teach yourself to bake a cake – much more pleasant than stopping and smelling what emanates from under your duvet if you use your time off to languish in your pit!

On the other hand, if you'd planned to have a much-needed life laundry on your day off (or at least tidy up the dirty knickers and empty chocolate wrappers that have lain under the bed for six months), read on. In the next chapter we'll consider why we should wave a Marigold-free hand bye-bye to doing our household chores, and live a little instead!

Modern Dilemma

Dear Modern Maiden,

I'm told nobody likes a grass, which is all very well when you're not feeling hard done by. I work in a young office, where the unwritten rule is 'work hard, play hard'. Fine, if you are one of my slack-arsed colleagues who calls in sick at the drop of a hat (or an E) after a heavy night, but since I am the only one in the office who maintains some semblance of professionalism, I end up doing all the work. Should I tell my boss that the mysterious bug that is doing the rounds in our office for the third time this year is none other than self-inflicted 'disco fever'?

Yours exhaustedly,

Amy

Dear Amy,

It must be tough bearing the brunt of your colleagues' slapdash attitudes, but I wouldn't go squealing to your boss just yet. I can only assume that she/he is aware of their behaviour and is turning a blind eye, unless she/he is suddenly going to come down on them like a ton of bricks at their annual appraisal. For now, I would catch a little disco fever myself – if you can't beat 'em, join 'em!

Yours conspiratorially,

MM

CHAPTER NINE

A Woman's Work Is Never Done, or: Housework and How to Avoid It

'A man may work from sun to sun but a woman's work is never done.' This never-ending nature of 'women's work' resonates as much today as it did during the Middle Ages. From the tenth to the fourteenth centuries, a man's work would have kept him busy, from sunup to sundown, toiling away in the fields or, if he was lucky, in a specialist trade, such as baking or carpentry. During this time, women would often sweat it out alongside their men-folk, albeit for a lesser wage (even when carrying out the same work) until the end of the working day, when 'women's work' would begin, namely the responsibilities of child-rearing and household tasks.

Jumping in my writer's time capsule to cross the five hundred years or so to the beginning of the twenty-first century, we might mutter with a Gallic shrug, 'plus ça change'. Even in these times of supposed equality, not only does 'women's work' conjure up images of mundane household chores rather than a spunky, exciting job, but we ladies still seem to suffer from what feminists have called 'the double burden'. That is, if and when we do decide to have children, we suffer the double whammy of a day's paid employment added to the lioness's share of the housework and childcare. Even today, it could be argued that men who do 'women's work' are perceived as being a mite effeminate, and that they only do it if they want to prove they can do it better.

If you want evidence, we only need take a quick peek at the depiction of men in advertising for cleaning products. Here we find that a fella who dons a pair of Marigolds will only do so if he is either 'hilariously' dressed up in drag as a caricature of an old fishwife, so scrawny that he could almost be mistaken for a puny wee lady (the point being, he has been emasculated simply by using the product), or telling his silly old 'Mrs' that she is too daft to have bought the right laundry detergent. The irony here is that, even as these adverts show an utter lack of respect for women (because they have been dreamed up in the main by men), we ladies still have to go out and buy the products (because our partners and husbands won't).

Sadly, men's attitudes to routine household chores, it would seem, are harder to shift than a stubborn biological stain. Yes, we ladies sure are taken to the cleaners when it comes to the time and energy we expend on housework while men, on the other hand, don't see or deal with dirt. They only make it. We could further argue that, weirdly, we ladies feel responsible for the household cleaning, so that even if a male in your house is prepared to get his hands dirty, we end up taking charge and telling him what needs doing and when. (Or if we reach a stalemate and our home is a filthy pit, we'll be the ones who throw our hands up in surrender and make that call to the cleaning agency.) Results from another of my random and hastily conceived mini-surveys show that it is clearly women who still perform the majority of household tasks and, even if both adults in the household work full-time, the responsibility for these tasks still falls (with the inevitability of the dishwasher breaking down on Christmas Day) the way of the lady of the house. Possibly, even if we know this is slightly nuts, we do this because a woman is often judged on whether she 'keeps a nice house', whether she is a stay-at-home mother, a working mum, or there is a man at home doing the stay-at-home father bit.

THE DIRTIEST WORD

If a woman falls into the first category above, what should I call her nowadays? If some people got their way, I shouldn't even use the word that has been employed since the thirteenth century to describe women who perform this function, but brace yourselves, ladies, I'm about to utter the most ugly profanity you'll find in this book. House-wife. There. I've said it. Forgive me. For there are some old-school feminists who would maintain that 'housewife' is as offensive as 'nigger',[49] and thereby, we could glean, more insulting to women than 'slut' or one of the ickiest expressions I could ever bring myself to utter, 'beef curtains'.[50]

But is 'housewife' as universally offensive and derogatory as some would have us believe? Originally, when first used in the 1200s, it had a neutral, literal meaning, as someone who stayed at home to run the household and happened to be a wife. It suffered a slight set-back in Victorian times, when housewives were considered immoral spend-thrifts who couldn't be trusted to look after their husband's money. (Perhaps we should rename WAGs, just plain old-fashioned house-wives in this case, or how about creating a new acronym, HAGs?) Attitudes to the word see-sawed in the last century, from the positive spin put on it by the super hausfrau of the 1950s, with all her new-found time and labour-saving devices, to the negative undercurrent it attained in the 1960s and 70s, when a more liberal zeitgeist told us the word belittled women and indicated their oppression by men.[51] As we arrive in the twenty-first century, society seems to be split between those women who would like to reclaim the word and those who find it outdated with negative connotations, if not going as far as to find it offensive. In fact, most women who responded to my mini-survey thought the latter, and even if they performed the role of a housewife, they'd prefer to be called anything but (preferring to be identified with the profession they had before they gave up work to care for small kids, or any part-time job they have).[52]

49 Germaine Greer, 'The Whole Woman' (Anchor Non-fiction) p.166
50 A term used by some eejits to describe a woman's genitals, which I find debasing and insulting in the extreme.
51 For this brief history of the etymology of the word housewife, I listened to Radio Four's Women's Hour. You can listen again at: http://www.bbc.co.uk/radio4/womanshour
52 Of thirty people surveyed, there were ten who performed this role, and only two who thought the term did not have negative connotations.

As for the men I sent the survey to, most did not respond, and the ones that did failed to answer the question on the word housewife. (Evidently surveys are like the washing-up and can be left for another day!) Those who did reply managed to cobble some sort of answers together, albeit jokily, when it came to 'househusband', a recent term used simply to describe a housewife's male counterpart. Yes, rather than giving thoughtful answers and confronting a contemporary real-life issue, the fellas commented antagonistically about how they would love to be househusbands and stay at home all day to watch TV or play computer games. Flippant answers aside, many people in the survey thought househusband has a positive ring to it, most thinking it 'groovier' than housewife and conjuring up an image of a man from a modern, liberal family. So, like 'stud' and 'slag' before them, two words that basically have the same meaning have taken on different nuances for the two genders, the male version being more positive than the female.

If the term housewife is outdated and disliked, and the term house-husband unfairly positive, how then should we define those who stay at home and look after young children, and do the best – or should that be worst – part of the household chores? The most common preference among those surveyed was for stay-at-home mum or stay-at-home dad. But could we not jazz things up a little and call ourselves house man-agers, a word which is not gender-specific and brings to mind a more professional occupation? We could, but we'd probably feel a bit of an arse. Or what about terms used by those who want to glam up the role, and who aspire to be 'domestic goddesses' or 'power moms'? These women maintain that the role has skills akin to those you will find in the workplace, such as time and money management and multi-tasking, and that it's not just about standing at the sink washing dishes. Perhaps, but that seems to gloss over the seemingly endless list of mundane tasks stay-at-home mothers carry out – a list of tasks so thankless that if the job were advertised in a newspaper, no one in their right mind would apply. As a stay-at-home mother, you are on call 24/7, get no sick days or annual leave, you are expected to cook, clean, tidy, look after the family's health, wardrobe (buying, laundering and repair thereof) and education, as well as all the household bills and shopping. All for the princely income of zero, nada, nichts. Domestic goddess? More like domestic slave.

Come on, my mop-loving maidens, isn't it time we admitted that no matter what we call ourselves, housework is boring, repetitive and about as intellectually stimulating as a soggy dishcloth? (I'm not saying this work should not be valued by society, but let's not pretend it is anything more than it is.) Shouldn't we agree that it makes no difference what we call the role of the person who looks after the household affairs, that unlike your gleaming bath taps, you can't polish a shit and make it shine? Anyway, no matter what we call ourselves, I say it's time we made a clean (or rather, dirty) break of it and put a stop to our preoccupation with keeping things spick and span. I'm not suggesting that we should live like slobs and throw in the (tea) towel on doing any housework at all, but simply that we should not spend so much time trying to create the perfect home, and live a little instead! Maybe then we could go some way to achieving the so-called 'work/life balance' so precious to us in the modern age. But how to do this when we have the pressures of work, home and children and we are poverty stricken in terms of time-wealth?

HOW TO BE A MIDDEN-FREE MAIDEN

Not wishing to throw up problems without offering a solution, and now that we've done the necessary pro-feminist bit, let's lighten the mood (and your washing load) a little, with the Midden-free Maiden's top ten tips for coping with the mountains of housework, dirty knickers, nappies and anything else life and our screaming kids throw at us.

1   If you can afford it, pay a cleaner. And pay them well, mind you. We're not talking about exploiting anyone for the sake of you living

like Lady Not-Muck! If you think you can't afford it, have a rethink, as what you may lose in a financial sense you will gain in precious time and sanity. If you add up the woman (or if you're lucky, man) hours spent in your home cleaning, or arguing over cleaning, you'll soon realise that the cost of having a cleaner is, ahem, dirt cheap.

2   Do your weekly food shop on the internet, especially if you have kids. Why anyone in this day and age would choose to wander around a vast supermarket, becoming trapped in a labyrinth of a squillion different products (all made by the same parent company), then lugging your mostly unwanted goods 1km to your parking space, only to discover your children have shoplifted a chocolate bar displayed at just the right height for little grabby hands, God only knows. Doing your grocery shopping on the internet means you can stick to a budget, won't be tempted to buy the bakery goods whose smell wafts temptingly around the store, and complete it in a matter of minutes. Enough said.

3   Household chores should be divvied up amongst everyone who lives there. (Pets being the exception, and since they only bring extra work, and unless you have a penchant for cleaning up animal puke and poo, perhaps you should boot them out completely.) This includes

children if you have them – even the smallest members of the family can help with the daily chores. For instance, your toddler can help sort laundry into different colours, thus multi-tasking as you teach them colour differentiation at the same time as doing the washing!

4   Don't buy dry-clean or hand-wash only garments, especially for chldren. (By the time you've taken them to the dry cleaners or reclaimed them from the bottom of the wash basket, they'll be wearing the next size up.) Don't wear then wash – use the sniff test to see if a garment is ready for laundering. (Only when you recoil and start retching should you set the washing machine to go!) As for ironing, apart from shirts and a few cotton items, this is an unnecessary task. So if I catch any of you ironing your sheets or

undergarments, I'll be sending for the men in grubby white coats. (They represent sanity, see, and don't feel the need for a whiter than white boil wash!)

5   When moving home, leave what is in your loft/garage/boxes stashed under the bed, just there. (Who knows, the next inhabitant may find something useful among your knick-knacks; if you want evidence of how much we love other people's crap we only need think of the global success of eBay.) The fact that you have been carting said baggage around since you left home aged eighteen does not make it necessary to schlep it unthinkingly to a dark and dusty corner of your next abode: if you haven't read it, viewed it, worn it, or used it since you last moved home – dump it!

6   Keep one room in your house as a sanctuary from the cleanliness we so insist on in our homes nowadays. As you walk through the (preferably hidden) door to this room, think of yourself as Alice in Wonder – or rather Waste – land, going to a magical place where you can dump dirty laundry and festering dishes should any unexpected callers drop by. If the doorbell rings and you feel ashamed of what's on show, rather than sorting through the detritus scattered across the four corners of your home, simply bung everything in your hidey-hole of horrors and sift through it later. (Much later …)

7   A note on carpets. If possible, avoid them completely and opt for wooden flooring instead. If you must have something soft under-foot, do not choose a carpet that is too light or too dark, and move furniture around often to avoid expensive cleaning bills/suspicious stains/ having to vacuum.

8   When having people to stay, remind yourself (and them) of an old Chinese proverb: Houseguests are like fish; after three days they start to smell! If you must entertain, don't wait on your guests hand and foot, rather work *their* fingers to the bone, and divvy up tasks among all of them. The bossier you are, the less likely they are to return next year!

9   Move to a hotel. The simple-yet-expensive option for avoiding housework altogether. We can but dream!

10   Promise yourself half an hour in a day where you simply sit, doing nothing. We were not put on this earth to be constantly polishing, wiping and dusting, and if we were, somebody is having a very bad joke at our expense. Life is too short for all this hygienic hysteria. I'm serious now, ladies.

For our final thoughts on the matter, let's go back the wonderful world of advertising. We've seen how men become namby-pamby big girls' blouses, if they so much as pick up a duster, but what about the portrayal of women in these usually cretinous ads? Whether it's new mums whose only worry when friends come over to see the new baby is whether their toilet smells bad, or little girls fawning over their mothers' soft dishwashing hands, when we view these commercials we must remind ourselves that women's brains are filled with more interesting things than soap suds! Not that I think you take these ads seriously, my slovenly sisters, but lest you need a reminder, do try not to become anxious if a pal pops in for a pee and your toilet isn't emitting daisy fresh smells. It's a toilet, after all!

Let's think back now to a little to earlier in this chapter when I mentioned that Victorian housewives were considered squandering spendthrifts who could not be trusted to look after the household finances. A shudder of recognition may have run through you when reading this as you contemplated your own financial misfortunes. Lest this is you, the next chapter has money-saving tips and tricks, ideas for budgeting and blagging, and info on what to do when money woes make you come to blows with your nearest and dearest!

Modern Dilemma

Dear Modern Maiden,

Recently my boyfriend came out with the following classic example of male stupidity, 'Did you know that there's a cobweb hanging in the bathroom which has been there for several weeks?' Needless to say, my reply was something too rude to put into print. This comment escalated into an enormous row as I suggested perhaps he could have got rid of said cobweb instead of moaning to me about it. His retort was, 'I've got my job, and you have yours.' I am at my wits end, as even though I have to look after my kids (they have a different dad) and most of the household affairs, I also have a part-time job and would appreciate a little help with the housework. Any ideas?

Yours truly,

Mary

Dear Mary,

You really need to get your house in order, and by that I don't mean the dusting in the bathroom. Good on him if he sees that the work you do in the house is a job, just like his, so then I hope he will agree that you are allowed benefits, like he no doubt has. The main one I am referring to being the right to strike: if I were you, I would lay down tools and forget about doing any housework at all for the next few weeks. Hopefully he'll soon realise that a little cobweb, compared to stained toilets, over-flowing bins and piles of unwashed laundry, pales into insignificance, and offer to help out more often. If he doesn't, I wouldn't rush to take out the rubbish, and simply bin him instead!

Yours no-nonsensely,

MM

CHAPTER TEN
Money Matters

'Keeping up with the Joneses' has been in common parlance since the post-war boom period when, for the first time in history, most of us in the Western world had disposable income to spend on the finer things in life.[53] Back in those days, this meant coveting your neighbour's TV as entire communities sat squashed together in front of the only 'box' on the street and domestic rivalry centred around whether you had a vacuum cleaner or washing machine, not whether you had the latest model.

Fast forward a couple of generations and, as new gadgets are foisted upon us at ever more alarming rates, we find it nearly impossible to keep up with ourselves, never mind with the Joneses. Anti-capitalists are troubled when manufacturers devise strategies to make us dig deep into our pink purses, lest we ladies are left cold by technological advances. They would say that the pastel-coloured MP3 players, female-orientated computer games (the ones without the killing, the cars or the sport) and pretty metallic mobile phones on offer are a well-thought out plan to manipulate us into buying things we don't usually have a yen, dollar or pound for. What's more, the media never tires of chastising us gals for apparently aspiring to a luxury lifestyle, setting our hearts and sights on sunny holidays, dining out and fancy designer clothes as never before.

---

53 In the States these halcyon days covered pretty much the 1950s onwards. Europe took a little longer to catch up and enjoyed these fruitful times in the Swinging Sixties. And in Australia the 'long boom' covered the period from the beginning of Second World War to the early Seventies, when standards of living nearly doubled.

It could be argued that with more of us than ever spiralling into a vortex of debt, these anti-consumerists are simply making good sense rather than being penny-pinching spoilsports. But don't think I am trying to rain on your (shopping) parade, my materialistic maidens! I'm not saying we should bid a tatty-gloved farewell to the joy of acquiring new things, and I wouldn't deny that shopping can be one of life's pleasures, even better, some may say, than sex. But let's agree to put the brakes on our spending before it is too late and we have a financial crash! Let's accept that we should be steady with our readies during the lean times in life and learn not to flash the cash when financial times are tough.

THE FINANCIAL YEAR

One way in which we can keep any eye on our finances is to take an annual audit of our expenditure and income (much like most companies and governments do) and see whether our own personal books balance. If that all sounds a bit too much of a hassle, why not take five minutes to complete the following financial health check and then see what the Modern Maiden prescribes for your financial ailments?

Quiz: Which financial season are you?

Question One

A week before pay day, I:

a Have more than a few pennies left over for a little treat or to put into my savings account.

b Pay day? I don't have a job but money's not an issue for me: I inherited a fortune from a distant relative.

c May need to borrow from friends or family. Mind you, I did that last month and haven't paid them back yet, so living like a hermit and eating nothing but cereal for a week might be my only option.

Have called my bank manager in floods of tears and am bouncing cheques all over the place, etc, etc.

Question Two

It's my best friend's birthday, and I plan to:

a Lavish her with attention, as well as a thoughtful, yet inexpensive gift.

b Throw her a party but write the guest list myself to ward off any freeloaders.

c Apologise and let her know I can't afford a gift but that I'll join her for birthday drinks, only to show off and buy a magnum of champagne when I'm a little merry.

d Spare no expense, and splurge my last few pennies or cents on something suitably flashy.

Question Three

When quarterly bills arrive I'm filled with:

a Surprise. I pay them by monthly by direct debit and should not be receiving paper bills.

Disgust. Daddy was meant to get all invoices and bills redirected to his place. Perhaps he needs to see a doctor about this memory?

c Indifference. I'll just stuff them into a drawer and wait for the final demands to arrive.

d Deep-seated angst. If I settle them I won't be able to buy the season's must-have coat. Now, where did I put that credit card?

Question Four

When it's my turn to buy a round of drinks:

a I'll buy everyone a small glass of wine or half measure, and a soft drink for myself, in case I have to get another round in later.

b Get everyone a double using my boyfriend's credit card.

c Splash out on a bottle of champers, knowing I'll have to get a bus instead of a cab home.

d Splash out on a bottle of champers, then think, 'What the heck. Taxi!'

Question Five

Charity begins:

a Once a month with a small amount to my favourite benevolent fund.

b At home … it's practically a crisis on a global scale how shabby my winter wardrobe is.

c Next year when I have paid off my debts.

d It depends. If there is a charity fashion event coming up, I'll tootle along to get myself seen.

Your answers

Mostly As – Spring

There is blossom on your money tree and your financial outlook is bright. You sensibly rain gifts on your friends and family in intermittent April showers, rather than in a torrential downpour, and you have money put by for a rainy day besides. However, perhaps you err a little too much on the financial side of caution, and as the spring days lighten, maybe your attitude to money could a little, too! Try to enjoy your hard-earned cash, because you deserve it, my frugal friend.

Mostly Bs – Summer

You are as generous with money as the summer sun is with her rays. With other people's money, that is. While there is no harm making hay while the sun shines if you have profited from an inheritance or windfall, remember that there is a certain satisfaction to be had in earning an honest crust yourself. Moreover, as the summer days are long, so is the rest of your life, so you should make sure your good fortune lasts as long as you do.

Mostly Cs –Autumn

The leaves are falling gently off your money tree, and you may feel you are losing your grip on your finances. You have monetary good intentions but blow it (in more ways than one) with impulse buying and generally sparing no expense. Do bear in mind that you reap what you sow financially, and that you will improve on your cash harvest if you squirrel a little away each month.

Mostly Ds – Winter

You wish it could be Christmas – and the January sales – every day, as you are the girl who can't stop spending. Unable to take pleasure in the simple things in life, you'd turn up your nose at a gift of a single snow-drop, preferring instead to splurge on a whole garland of winter flowers. Be warned, my feckless fritterer: unless you take a season to hibernate your credit cards and cheque books, your finances could become a permanent winter of discontent!

MORE SQUALOR THAN DOLLAR

Indeed, what to do if you end up in this bleak situation, living with more squalor than dollar in your life? The perhaps unwelcome answer is that Rome wasn't built in a (pay) day, so if you have bad debts it will take time and effort to work your way back to solvency. But it can be done. When you are desperate, your thoughts may turn to the old adage 'beg, borrow and steal' in order to survive, but a more realistic method of sorting out your finances could be to blag, budget and reveal. Easier said than done? Let the money-conscious maiden show you the way.

Blag

It's not strictly true that the best things in life are free, but you're flat broke, so should you be hankering after the best things in life, anyway? Never fear, it is possible to get stuff for free using the gentle art of blag-ging. From the French, blaguer, to lie, this basically means talking your way into acquiring new things without having to pay for them.

❀ If you are in dire need of a haircut, many salons offer freebies if you are willing to let a student loose on your locks! And speaking of students, student canteens are subsidised so if you have a college or university near your home or work (and you are not already legitimately attending), you could try blagging your way into one for a cheap and nutritious meal. (And who knows what friendly young chap you may lock eyes with over the spicy bean burgers?)

● Lots of supermarkets offer three-for-two on certain products. Do exploit these offers, even if it means eating nothing but a nasty flavour of soup (oxtail, for instance) for weeks on end or using a blonde shampoo even if you're a ravishing redhead. (Come to think of it, this might be a good experiment to see if there is actually a difference between these two allegedly colour-specific products.) Beggars literally can't be choosers.

● If you haven't been out for months due to a lack of lolly, you could try to blag your way onto a guest list in a nightclub. Ring them, speaking in a confident tone, and tell them you are starting a new local paper and would like to review the club, or put on a foreign accent and say you are from the leading club website in Paris, Milan or Tokyo. If this fails, you could try turning up on the night and sweet-talking the bouncers. Top tip: best to wear your sluttiest clothes to do so, as bouncers aren't known for their discretion.

● If you live somewhere swell (by the sea or in a touristy city, for instance) and it's been a long time since your last foreign holiday, you could try a holiday house swap. There are lots of agencies and websites set up for this activity, but be sure to use a reputable one as you don't want to come home to fewer possessions than you already have.

● There is a plethora of money-saving websites, offering price comparisons for utilities companies and products, but also giving tips where to find money-off vouchers for popular stores. A little detective work on these sites could help solve the case of your missing fortune, so it's worth taking the time to investigate.

Budget

When on the breadline, living hand-to-mouth is a necessity, as is not spending more than you earn. You need to set to work with a realistic monthly budget, including hidden costs, otherwise known as the costs you don't want to face up to, including interest on your credit card(s)/long overdue debts to family and friends/the unpaid tab at your local bar – these all still count. Nobody wants to appear a money-grubber, but at the same time, you will have to be thrifty if you are ever to make headway with your debts. The must-dos of living on a budget are:

- Resist the urge to splurge. If you must have a mooch around the shops, only take a certain amount of cash with you in order to avoid impulse buys, and leave your credit cards at home.

- It might pay to be drastic with the plastic, and destroy any credit and store cards you own. Alternatively, hide them somewhere in the darkest corners of your house. Then, by the time you remember where you put them you'll have had a chance to reflect on whether you need to spend money that day.

- Learn to say 'no' to a night out with friends if you can't afford it, or suggest you do something cheap. If you must go out, take a certain amount of cash with you and, again, leave the cards at home. If you do run out of cash, there's no harm in trying to blag drinks off friendly looking guys. (But keep your eyes peeled for any dodgy-tasting or funny-coloured liquids, because you don't want your successful blagging to come at a price, after all!)

- We gals love to cut back on our food, so why not think of this as a new kind of diet, a financial one? Not to get into that little black dress, but back into the black ... full stop!

Reveal

If the only thing you are economical with is the truth about your debts, it's probably time to come clean about them. Burying your head (and your unpaid bills) in the sand, rather than facing up to what you owe, might mean it takes you years to get back on the financial road to recovery. It's no good being creative with your own accounting, my wasteful welshers, as it's only you who will suffer a sort of financial food poisoning from cooking your own books!

Having admitted your financial woes to yourself, it's now time to take action, and you should visit a financial advisor for the best way out of your monetary misery. Your bank manager, too, should receive a visit, but don't let her fool you into a loan: this is not always the best or quickest way out of debt. If you are in a relationship, the most difficult aspect of revealing your debt may be fessing up to your partner. Not that there is much hope. Indeed it is often quoted that one in three of us lies about our finances to our partners, and we're told that money worries are one of the biggest causes of arguments or divorce. Like all aspects of your relationship, the answer is to be truthful from the outset. And if he's the one who's bad with money, ask him to let you take control of the joint account, especially if you have a shared mortgage, or else you may lose your, um, joint!

In this chapter we have seen that a financial problem shared is a problem – if not a debt – halved. More importantly, I hope we've seen that owning spangly new possessions, cars and houses is less important than owning (as in taking responsibility for) our finances themselves. Indeed, in times where many women end up living in poverty after they divorce, or in old age, as boring as it may sound, it is never too early to start thinking about getting your finances in order and saving for your future, notably for your pension. (And no, I'm not talking about buying a small boarding house in France or Italy; I mean saving money for your retirement.) Because while women earn less than men, and while staying at home looking after the kids does not offer a pension or even a wage, there's no denying the importance of taking control of your finances and not letting your spending habits, or indeed the credit companies and banks, control you!

Modern Dilemma

Dear Modern Maiden,

I'm confused regarding money etiquette on dates, and get flustered (and irate) when it comes to the end of an evening if my date insists on paying. Sometimes I think I have appeared downright rude or even mad as I have tried to stuff wodges of cash into prospective boyfriends' wallets. But I do feel strongly that him paying for me means he expects some sort of payment in kind. If you know what I mean.

Yours,

Yvonne

Dear Lacking in Going-Dutch Courage,

I know exactly what you mean. You want to pay your way but don't want to appear ungracious about it. And I'd agree that where dating is concerned, there is perhaps no such thing as a free lunch or dinner, and lovin' kindness may be expected in return. But isn't it your date's problem if you don't put out after he's shelled out? Alternatively, perhaps you should not be so suspicious and take his offer at face value; after all, if a friend offered to pay for dinner, wouldn't you think of it as a pleasant treat? Besides, you could always offer to pay the next time, handily bringing up the subject of a second date if you like the look of him!

Yours generously,

MM

Dear Modern Maiden,

I don't wish to appear stingy, but I'd like your advice on how I broach the subject of joint finances with my boyfriend. His love of trendy clothes, records and fancy meals knows no bounds, but his wallet certainly doesn't. Within a week of payday his wages are more or less spent, and he only has enough for the bare essentials until the following month. I do earn more than him but I'm now left in a position where if I fancy a simple trip to the cinema, or even a bottle of wine, it always has to be my shout. It is getting quite embarrassing, particularly in front of our friends. Do you have any ideas?

Yours sincerely,

Kathy,

Dear Kathy,

You do not say whether you live together, so let's assume you do. In the long term, a joint account might be the solution to your problems, but in the meantime, since your boyfriend can't be trusted, why not suggest he puts in a certain amount each month to cover rent, bills and incidentals into your account and you can manage all the mundane household affairs? I don't think it's necessarily embarrassing that you end up paying for him in this day and age, but perhaps there might be fun in trying to cut back on things together?

Yours frugally,

MM

CHAPTER ELEVEN
Make Friends, Make Friends, Never, Ever Break Friends

Life is full of mysteries, which range from the downright weird (Why do men have nipples?) to the mind blowing (Why are we here?). We humans love to ponder these unexplained phenomena and come up with big and supposedly clever theories to get to the bottom of things. At times these theories are indeed well thought out, and present a case for us being superior to the other life forms on the planet, but at other times we simply make up supernatural claptrap that makes us seem about as intelligent as a sea slug.[54]

One mystery that has long since baffled scientists is whether or not animals have friendships. At first glance it would seem that primates (our closest relations in the animal kingdom) do, based literally on a 'you scratch my back, I'll scratch yours' reciprocal relationship. Scientists would claim that this mutual grooming by chimps among non-kin, the primping and preening one another in return for support if one of the gang gets into fight, is proof enough that animals can have friendships of sorts.[55] We could argue that these activities are mirrored by human behaviour: just imagine the ritual of a gang of gals, getting ready for their Friday night out, styling one another's hair and doing each other's make-up, before hitting the streets, bars and clubs. Then, later on, if one of the gang gets involved in a round of alcohol-fuelled fisticuffs, the others are sure to wade in to stick up for her. Handbags at dawn, ladies! Joking aside, scientists find it harder to explain the altruism involved in this behaviour and what motivates us humans to

54 For example, the Creationist theory that fossils were put on earth by God as part of a cunning plan to confuse the fuck out of us.

55 Source: 'Science News,' Volume 164, No. 18, November 1, 2003 online.

make close attachments than they do those of our furry friends. More baffling still, to them and everybody else, are the spider's web-like intricacies of same-sex female friendships.

Strange then, that while there are thousands upon thousands of books analysing the psychology behind our dating and sex lives, there are comparatively few which occupy themselves with the delicate nature of same-sex female friendships.[56] Yes, the subject has been handled on a fictional basis in film and literature but usually only from one of two black and white perspectives: the slushy sisterly solidarity of *Thelma and Louise* types, or back-stabbin' bitches portrayed in films such as *Heathers* or any other high school teen movie you'd care to think of. Not that there isn't some truth in the romanticised view that the strong bonds between women can be more rewarding (and last longer) than an intimate male/female relationship. Equally, let's not deny that women can be fiercely competitive in their friendships, and can sometimes sell each other out quicker than you can say 'cute guy', but the reality is a shade, or rather shades, in between these monochrome polar opposites.

And what an artist's palette of shades in between we gals create. There are the times when we suffer from the green-eyed monster if a pal gains status because of her new job, or she goes through a physical transformation, from Plain Jane to gorgeous babe, and the joyous times when we go through a purple patch and a new-found friend becomes our closest ally and confidante. There's also when we're feeling yellow, too cowardly to tell an old chum when we feel they've let us down for one reason or another. This rainbow of feelings can be as painful and joyful as any sexual relationship we'll ever have, and, as such, we will start this relationship section of the book on how to keep your female relationships in the pink, and when to reveal your true colours if a friend is making you see red. Finally, lest you thought I'd forgotten we are living in the modern age, we will take a brief foray into the world of platonic male/female friendships, ranging from your ambiguous relationship with the boy next

56 On Amazon.co.uk at the time of writing, there are 4419 titles on sexual relationships and only 579 on friendships.

door to the somewhat antiquated and unpleasant concept of being a 'fag hag'.

ANIMAL MAGIC

Let's return first to the animal kingdom for a menagerie of comparisons of the different types of female friends we may come across throughout our lives. We'll look at how to tame these beasts if they get out of control, put them in quarantine if they're acting up, or set them free, depending.

The lady dawg or bitch

She tries to undermine you in a variety of situations and makes the most of it if you are having a bad hair – not to mention, weight, romance or any other kind of bad – day. She may disguise her bitchiness with backhanded compliments, like, 'That dress is gorgeous! It hides the extra weight you've put on recently.' But it's not only you who receives the occasional tongue-lashing from her. She bad-mouths other friends in your pack and has the competitive spirit in spades, bigging up her own achievements and belittling everyone else's. It's a cliché, but a lack of self-confidence probably lies at the root of her ill-will, and if she has any redeeming features, it may be worth trying to get her to recognise it. Tread carefully when you approach her, though: her bite may be worse than her bark!

The clucking hen

She's your worry-wart chum, who you can call at the drop of a hat if you have a problem, but with the proviso that she will make a mountain out of the smallest molehill. Try to take her advice with a pinch of salt, as she will tend to over-dramatise your dilemmas (as well as her own), and will flap around to any bad news like a mother hen. She can be a control freak and won't like it if you don't return her calls or emails with an immediate affectionate and gushy reply. If her constant worrying bothers you, try to lighten her load with a joke and a smile, because if you simply tell her she's getting on your nerves, she may think she's reached the lowest of the low in your pecking order.

The queen bee

She is the undisputed leader of the pack. The other girls in your gang will buzz around her, as she strikes fear and admiration into their hearts with her stunning good looks, wit, charm and terrifying bossiness. On the plus side, she will attract fun, frolics and hopefully fellas into your group. On the other hand, you may feel she hogs the limelight, and that you never get a look-in if you have news, good or bad, to share. If her vainglorious-ness gives you a (queen) bee in your bonnet, you should question whether you feel insecure or envious of her status. If the answer is no, and she is simply selfish, then deal with her as you would an attacking insect: try to swat her away, ignore her, and if she continues to irritate you, exterminate her from your address book! If the answer is yes, it may be you who's insecure, so make sure you only see her when you're feeling sweet as honey, and avoid her on the days when you need a pick-me-up chum.

The chameleon

You might not recognise her if you passed her in the street, as she goes to great lengths to blend in with today's version of what's 'in', with no distinct style or even personality of her own. She is a yes-woman and you'll be left waiting if you want to hear her express any opinion other than the Zeitgeist or her love for the latest hot fashion or band. Don't be too quick to shy away from her company, though. Even if she's shallow and you feel you will never get to know her properly, it can be fun to be around someone without having to share your innermost thoughts, or listen to hers. Nonetheless, a word of warning: the chameleon can pick up new trends and looks from anywhere, and you don't want her to end up morphing into a version of you.

The faithful lapdog

She's the old school friend who reliably calls once a month, suggesting a catch-up, unperturbed by the fact you no longer have anything in common and your lives have taken different paths. You respect her loyalty and don't want to lose touch completely, but wish she would stop hanging on your every word, seemingly living vicariously through your success and achievements. Don't be too hard on her: your lives may be moving in different directions, but you share a lot of history and could still be on the same wavelength. You may find that if you distance yourself a little, and suggest meeting on a less-regular basis, the encounters will be more bearable. Or, who knows, you may find yourself enjoying them!

The predatory vixen

She's the most gorgeous gal in your gang – a real fox – but unfortunately, she needs every passing male to confirm this, and will even make passes at your male in order to prove it to herself! She ignores the unwritten rule that friends' partners become instantly untouchable, and she will do her best to sidle her way into his affections (only so he fancies her, nothing more), and will be heedless of the effect it will have on you and him. If you are single, and she sees someone catching your eye in a nightclub, she will muscle in on the act, shaking her tail in his direction and generally making a pain of herself. The best way to deal with her is to outfox her by thinking ahead. If you've got your eye on someone, put her off the scent and pretend you fancy his mate. And before she meets your main squeeze, warn him to give her the cold shoulder if he doesn't want to land in hot water!

The huggable husky

She is your best friend, the bosom bud who has been with you through the best and worst of times, and she knows the best and worst of you to boot. If you live far away from one another, you can pick up where you left off at the drop of a hat, and if she lives around the corner, you never sicken of seeing her. Like a husky, she is affectionate and works hard to keep your relationship going. That's not to say you don't have the occasional spat, but your relationship goes deeper than having sour grapes because she pinched your favourite lipstick in 1995. You've made a friend for life here, M'lady, so don't take her for granted, and give this huggable husky the attention and respect she deserves!

Needless to say, you might not recognise your friends in any of the above breeds, although you may begin to if we experiment with a little cross-breeding: The Husky mates with the Hen, to become your kindly, yet maddening, best friend, or the Queen Bee gets jiggy with the Bitch, to become everyone's worst nightmare. Either way, the point is: friends, like animals, can be tamed and any conflict in your friendships resolved without the flying of fur!

HOW TO MAKE FRIENDS

Making new friends is a little like giving birth: in an ideal world it should happen naturally and not be forced. In your early twenties, this is a doddle. Or, if we continue the birth analogy, meeting new people in your youth is as easy as popping out your fourth kid. At this age we have had time to buddy up with pals at university or college, or are starting out in our first job and can bond with similar new recruits at the shock of getting out of bed before midday and/or being told what to do. As we get older though, and especially if we have moved town for our careers or love, making friends can become trickier, as we just aren't exposed to the same bonding situations as before. (It's harder to make friends in the office when you are one doing the telling what to do!) This is the point where we may have to use the friendship equivalent of inducing a birth, forcing new attachments by any means possible! We all know the usual tips suggested by lifestyle manuals or magazines, such as joining a social club, using on-line friendship sites or practising platonic flirting, but the following fun activities will perhaps offer a quicker route out of solitary confinement.

- Start smoking, and if you already smoke, smoke more. There is no end to the possibilities for smokers to strike up a match, a conversation and, with luck, a friendship, i.e. having a smoke-break, cadging a ciggy or a lighter, and – depending on where you live – huddling together outside in wind, rain and storm. Yes, you may die quicker, but at least you'll have made more friends on your cancerous route to the big ashtray in the sky.

- Never decline an invitation, even if the event itself promises to be as dull as ditch water. You never know; you may hit it off with a mirror invitee who is equally under-whelmed by the whole thing. Oh, and if you live in the shadow of an extrovert partner, leave them at home for once, so that you get a chance to get a word in.

- If you are shy at social functions, ease (or should that be Es?) your way into conversation with the help of drink or drugs. And yes, I mean even if it is a coffee morning, brunch or any other occasion deemed unsuitable for such activity. But we're talking a cheeky snifter of your favourite liquor or sniff of your favourite powder for a little Dutch courage. You wouldn't want anyone to guess, would you? (Until you get to know them better!)

- As a last resort, have a baby. New mums have a toy-chest full of opportunities for meeting new people at the doctor's surgery, playgroup or at the swings in the park. But while it's easy to bond over the trials and tribulations of giving birth and raising young kids, you can't always expect these 'mummy friends' to develop into more meaningful relationships (in fact, as your kids get older your friendship may be left at the school gates).

- I know you are clever enough to work this one out, but the last two points, like drugs and booze, shouldn't be mixed. We're talking mothers', not AA, meetings.

- Finally, remember it's all about quality, not quantity. If you already have a lovely network of friends, why feel the need to make new ones? Instead, why not suggest having adventures with your old friends, such as trying a new sport, or going on holiday together? You may get to see a side of them (and you) you never knew existed.

DITCH THE BITCH

Mind you, sometimes the problem is reversed, and we tear our hair out as to how we can get rid of an unreliable, disloyal or irritating chum. Unfortunately, while there are millions of accepted methods for dumping a boyfriend, there are no social niceties for ditching the bitch in your life. Often, we just let the friendship drift away naturally by freezing her out, not returning her calls or emails, and hoping she'll eventually get the message. It is tad cruel, as she may think you're dead or have eloped, but, to be honest, if she does, so much the better – she won't be bothering you again! But what to do if she's previously been the faithful lapdog we met earlier in the chapter who has trans-mogrified into a stubborn Rottweiler, tugging at trouser leg, unwilling to give you up? If you don't fancy telling her outright why you want to blast her into your past, you could use the following methods for making friends in reverse, in order to get rid of her.

- Chain-smoke in the face of the non-smoking chum you wish to ditch, never asking permission if you can light up in her company, or even in her home. If she was previously your smoking bud, give up (or pretend to) and become the sanctimonious ex-smoker no puffer ever wants to be around.

- Decline all invitations from her, or from any mutual friends, for the time being. Let it slip to shared acquaintances that you've fallen out and hopefully they'll do your dirty work for you, asking her in all innocence, 'So why have you and … had a tiff?'

- Overdo your drug of choice either to piss her off or to get the bottle (geddit?) to tell her why you dislike her to her face.

- Again, you could always have a baby and then use the 'I'm too busy/sleep-deprived/the baby-sitter let me down' excuse not to see her. If this seems a little extreme, just dream one up. You've no intention of seeing her again, so she'll be none the wiser!

You might, however, want to reflect whether it is wise to exclude her from your social circle in the first place. For as you get older, this circle continues to decrease, and in time you may regret not simply getting to the bottom of why the two of you fell out. It often pays to be brave in these circumstances, and your friendship should be all the deeper and more rewarding for it.

MR PLATONIC

Mixed-sex friendships are an altogether different kettle of fish as, men being the simple folk they are, your relationship won't suffer from the vagaries and vicissitudes of an all-female friendship. That is, of course, unless your chum is gay, when (sorry to stereotype, but I do so with good reason) he could be more of a bitch than any of your girly chums. Speaking of which, the notion of being a 'fag hag', that is, a woman who likes to hang around gay men simply because they are gay, was clearly concocted by a homophobic misogynist. Firstly, we lasses (mostly) don't labour under the illusion that every heterosexual bloke we meet is going to pounce on us, and that every gay man won't, and secondly, our gay chums' appeal is based on their personalities, not their sexuality. Rant over.

That said, and without wishing to come across as a clichéd old hack, there is one problem that can rear its ugly head (yes, pun intended yet again) with male/female friendships: your hetero male friend may well try it on with you at some point. Whether he is motivated by a genuine appreciation of the wonder that is you, or because he's not had a lumber for several months and you are the nearest available female, should help you decide how to deal with his advances. For example, 'I am in love with you, always have been in love with you, always will be in love with you', should be treated rather more gently than, 'Let's have sex. What do you mean no? We're friends aren't we? Just think of it as body contact, like a massage.' The latter should be treated with disdain and a firm, 'No!' After all, if this is his attitude, the sex is hardly going to knock your socks off, is it? (And by the way, if you come onto him, don't be surprised if you are similarly rebuffed!)

Another thorny issue is the advisability of making new male friends if you are in a sexual relationship with a bloke already. If you're all adults, old male friends around before your relationship should be no threat to your new partner, but what about if you happen to hit it off with the new chap at work, behind the bar, or on the train home when you are three sheets to the wind? It all depends on how you deal with it. Inviting him back for coffee is not an option, it's an overture of a non-platonic kind and he'd be forgiven for thinking (but not for assuming) that you want more than just a latte. If he is also in a relationship, your chances for finding friendship are higher, notwithstanding jealous partners on either side. Perhaps now the Modern Maiden's mantra of 'laddy-like, but ladylike' can be used to best effect: if you act like one of the lads around him, your friendship could flourish, but remember to maintain a ladylike decorum which says, 'stay back' if things start to get a little fruity.

There is a playground poem from when I was a young slip of a thing (about ten years ago, give or take a decade!) that says: 'Make friends, make friends, never, ever break friends', but it's only recently that I found out the ending to this rhyme: 'And if you do you'll catch the flu and that will be the end of you.' A childish threat, perhaps, but one we would do well to remember if our friends have let us down, or are getting on our nerves. Friendships, like pets, aren't just for Christmas, or birthdays for that matter, to be wheeled out when you are trying to get the numbers up at a social gathering. Rather, like domestic animals, they need to be nurtured and looked after, and not sent back to the kennels immediately if they don't behave exactly as you expect them too!

Men, on the other hand, can sometimes just be for Christmas, if, for example, you don't want to attend that important function on your own, or you fancy having someone to snuggle up to during the cold festive season. The next few chapters in this relationship section of the book will be a no-holds-barred look at our relationships with men and how, contrary to the usual advice given to women, we can make the most of our sexual relationships simply by being ourselves!

Modern Dilemma

Dear Modern Maiden,

I'm not sure you could really call my dilemma a problem, but it is something that has been niggling away at me for a while now. I am starting to wonder if I am as close to a dear friend of mine as I'd thought. On the one hand, she always lends a helping hand if I'm in dire straits, or a shoulder to cry on if I've been a dumper or dumpee, but she never seems to be around during the good times. I almost feel like she takes pleasure when I'm miserable, and would prefer to be absent when I'm on the up and up!

Yours sadly,

Evie

Dear Evie,

My, you are right, it is unusual to have a foul – rather than fair – weather friend. On the one hand, it's great that she benevolently offers up various parts of her anatomy in times of trouble (a shoulder to cry on, a helping hand) but you're also right (if we continue the body imagery) that a good friend is someone whose leg you can pull, and who you kick up your heels with, too! It obviously makes her feel good to be around someone feeling low. It's up to you whether you make heavy of her foul-weather attitude, or ride the storm and appreciate the fact that you have someone there for you when you need them. Not everybody does!

Yours tempestuously,

MM

Dear Modern Maiden,

About a year ago, a good friend and I decided to share a flat, having both split up with long-term boyfriends around the same time. At first we were ideal flatmates: we spent drunken nights bemoaning our exes, kept our distance when we knew the other needed space, and perhaps, most importantly, she's an early bird and the bathroom was always free for me in the mornings! Then, the inevitable happened, and one of us got a new boyfriend. In this case, me. Now the jealous bint is moaning that he's round at ours the whole time, and is threatening to move out. I really wish she would so I could move my new boyf in. Have you any ideas how I could hurry this along?

Yours claustrophobically,

Claudia

Dear Three's-a-crowd,

I guess what you would like me to do is suggest ways you can 'space her out' quicker, i.e. make her so uncomfortable in her own home that she runs for the hills, pronto! Having him hang about naked, making loud sex noises and using up all the hot water for long, romantic bubble baths would all work in this regard. But what I am going to do is suggest you take a long look in the mirror and consider your selfish behaviour. Unless you own the place, you and your other half should stop wandering around like you do … and if you don't own the place, the best thing will be to talk things through and come to some agreement on how often your boyfriend can stay over. And if you like him that much that you must see him every day, why not stay at his place and give your friend a break?

Yours amicably,

MM

CHAPTER TWELVE
The Dating Game

Scrabble, chess, bingo. Three activities we do for amusement or pleasure, which generally bring us a feeling of bonhomie, and are also cheap, rarely emotionally scarring and even the sorest losers are never down for more than half an hour. Doctors tell us that the mental and emotional benefits of game playing help us live longer, happier, healthier lives … but most of all, games are fun. So the fool who took it upon themselves to call the act of deciding from one nerve-racking, toe-curlingly cringe-making meeting whether you are meant to be life partners a 'game', clearly never actually endured the torment of going on a date.

To think of an explanation, could it be the tactics involved, the poker faces we need to pull when our friend hooks us up with our 'perfect match' and he treats us like a perfect hooker? The feeling of victory if it goes okay, or humiliation if it doesn't? If we must compare the act of finding a date to a game, perhaps our best bet is one of hide-and-seek. We gals excitedly scream, 'Coming, ready or not!' while vast swathes of men try to hide away forever in eternal bachelorhood! Because despite the choices on offer with online dating, blind dating, personal ads, speed dating and the good old-fashioned method of simply asking someone out, finding a decent date can be as elusive as an honest personal ad or online personality profile.

Even if we do go out on a date, sometimes the ordeal is so boring, so embarrassing and sometimes so downright terrifying, that we wonder why we ever went on it in the first place. There are dating disaster stories on internet dating sites, in agony aunt and uncle columns and circulated by urban myth that would put *The Poseidon Adventure* to shame: from tales of your blind date running late and you just running away at the mere sight of him, to your squeeze expecting you to put out after asking you to put up the bill, to the inevitable horror stories of nerves getting the better of one or other of you, and the wrong kind of bodily functions playing a part in the fun and frolics (most commonly letting out violent and smelly farts at the most inopportune moment, just as you lean in for that first kiss). I almost wonder if we should declare dating, well, dated, and hark back to a time when we courted out of financial necessity, when romantic love was a mere twinkle in somebody's eye. During the eighteenth and nineteenth centuries, for example, for the middle classes at least, courtship was a formal event arranged according to hierarchy and social status. It's only in the last hundred years that people could conduct the gentle art of wooing in privacy again, without a chaperone or your mother sizing up your prospective beau's … wallet, dearies … wallet!

It's no surprise, then, that such a tricky subject should throw up – and why not continue the vomiting metaphor – such a sickening amount of dating guides and manuals dedicated to telling us how to find a date, how to act, and what to say on one, and what to do when a first date doesn't lead to a second. To name but a few, we can choose from *The Complete Book of Rules*, *The Real Rules*, *The New Book of Rules*, *Men Are From Mars, Women Are From Venus*, *He's Just Not That Into You* (etc. etc. etc. ad infinitum), each new book pooh-poohing the ethos of the previously most successful guide, and claiming new copper-bottomed guarantees for success in the world of love and dating.

Come on, girls! Isn't it time that we were the ones to do the pooh-poohing? Shouldn't we be telling these airhead authors that their erroneous editions stink to high heaven, and consigning their misleading manuscripts to the scrap-yard of history? Shouldn't we fight back and let these writers know that we realise, despite their claims to the contrary, that they are all saying the very same thing:

❀ Listen exclusively to the author's advice and you will meet 'Mr

Right' and never have a dodgy date, short-lived relationship or bungled bunk-up ever again;

- It is the bloke who dictates how we should behave on a date and whether it went well – indeed, you are simply a passenger on his journey toward finding love;
- Whereas men cannot be condemned for sleeping around (it's in their nature), we women shouldn't do so, and if we do, we'll never find our 'perfect match'?

Pay attention, my sassy singletons, and I mean get really close and personal:[57] contrary to what we've been told by these pseudo-psychological scribblers, it's only by experiencing a few cock-ups (and cocks up us) that we can be equipped to know what we want from a relationship. Only by being true to ourselves and not by experimenting on some poor sod 'til we have a ring on our finger, can we find true happiness. Only by indulging in the occasional spot of sexual sorbet – that is, no-strings-attached sex to cleanse the sexual palette when coming out of a relationship – can we feel ready to move on to discover our next beloved. Strangely, these books seem to assume that we expect each and every one of our dates to be possible routes to meeting Mr Right, and they ignore the fact that, hell, he may not be 'that into you' but who said you're that into him either, but he'll do for now/for a much needed tumble in the hay/as a date for your best friend's wedding – take your pick!

Besides, if everyone lived by the same set of rules, life would be very boring, wouldn't it? Yes, these guides seem to forget that each of us is unique and where one – probably rather thick if you ask me – bloke may be tricked into a relationship by your following *The Rules*, another may be put off by your total lack of individuality (who knows, maybe he would like the real you?). Of course, I'm not denying that men and woman are different, and that some of us like a challenge and the games people can play. It's just that we're living in a real, not ideal, world, where dates are sometimes just for fun, where they can turn out badly, and people make mistakes and are all the more human for it. So, instead of following the advice offered in the usual fodder, why not use the following ideas for guidance and giggles, not as a set of rules to live your life by, as we have a bit of fun dispelling the myths from dating guides of old.

Myth One
Thou shalt ne'er initiate courtship with thine fair knight,
OR, YOU SHOULD NOT ASK A MAN OUT ON A DATE

So, you get on well and have shared a few drinks after work (albeit surrounded by ten other work colleagues) and he regularly compliments you. We need to kick into the long grass the outdated notion that he'll now ask you out. Maybe (and men tell me this is the case more than you might think) he finds you so knee-tremblingly gorgeous that he wouldn't dare, or maybe – for now – he just thinks of you as a friend. Maybe he is slightly put off by that cold sweat you break into every time he speaks to you. Whatever. If you have a fancy to bag that guy you … um, fancy, why not take the plunge and be the one to ask him out? If he says yes, you 'merely' have to dazzle him over the course of the date with your natural charm and exuberance. He's hardly going to avoid a second date, as some ludicrously out-of-touch dating guides would have us believe, simply because you (supposedly) emasculated him by taking the first step. If he had fun, he'll come back for more. On the other hand, he might say no. But you do have a valid passport and cash in the bank, right? So, there is nothing stopping you fleeing the country at a moment's notice if you can't deal with the rejection!

Myth Two
Thine chastity belt must remain securely locked at the beginning of the courtship,
OR, DON'T SLEEP WITH HIM WITHIN THE FIRST FEW WEEKS, LET ALONE ON THE FIRST DATE

Fifty years of supposed sexual liberation and now this, as the authors of the aforementioned and afore-slated dating books would have us believe that promiscuity doth not to a relationship lead! It's time to be blunt, my bed-hopping beauties … if you fancy him, and he fancies you, why not show willing and get him to show you his (forgive me) willy at the first opportunity? The alternative is you snatch a few dates here and there without him getting anywhere near your (again, I apologise) snatch, only to find out three months down the line that your sexual chemistry is as explosive as the junior science set you got for Christmas when you were ten.[58] What's more, how else, other than by sleeping around, will you discover who and what lights your fire in the bedroom? I mean, think back to your first love. You thought it was fireworks at the time, but you realise now it was little more than the second-rate sizzle of one of those indoor sparkler thingummies. And finally, if you think you will get a bad reputation, you can always pre-empt any misogynistic mutterings with the following firm, yet (un)fair, denial, 'There was no way I was going to sleep with that guy, he was all arse and no cock!' Shameless yet blameless, remember!

Myth Three
Thou shalt cut off thine nose to spite thine face,
OR, NEVER GIVE HIM THE BENEFIT OF THE DOUBT

If, for instance, he rattles his way through your first date, chattering more than a pair of non-stop comedy false teeth, and yet he remains almost alluring in spite of this loquaciousness (or he does not seem to be the biggest loser on the planet and it's been a while since your last close encounter of the flirty kind), why not give him a second chance? I'm not saying this can't backfire though: one friend of mine was charmed throughout a dinner date, as her beau inundated her with sincere enough sounding questions about her family, friends and life thus far, only to discover at the end of the night that he had been using

---

58 A gift almost as disappointing as 'Mousetrap'. The game that takes ten hours to build and then, yes, all that really happens is : The. Mouse. Gets. Trapped. Sigh!

prompt cards hidden under his napkin (the poor nervous bastard had knocked over a drink, and she spied the cards as she helped him mop it up). Thinking that it was kind of cute he had gone to such an effort to woo her, she agreed to a second date, where one thing led to another, which in turn to led to the bedroom, where, yes, you guessed it, he also needed prompt cards in order to make his moves. Needless to say, this was a going a little too far to let things go any further!

Nonetheless, some dating handbooks seem to suggest that the Second Coming is more credible than second chances ought to be,[59] and that your date should be as perfect as the relationship that will inevitably follow. Frankly, I think it's bullshit. If you go on a second date and it confirms your misgivings of the first, don't go on a third, and if you are still wavering rather than being wowed, there is no harm in thinking, third time lucky. What have you got to lose?

Myth Four
Thou shalt not address him on the communication device known as the 'telephone',
OR, DON'T CALL HIM IF HE DOESN'T CALL YOU FIRST

So the rude so-and-so did not call you after the first date. It's not rocket science. He can't be bothered, he didn't fancy you that much, or he may genuinely have lost your number. Now, let's compare the dating experience to a job interview – you go all out, dressed to the nines, on your best behaviour and with your potty mouth expertly toilet-trained. But just as with a job interview, shouldn't we feel entitled to get 'feedback' on a date after all that effort we've gone to? If he doesn't want a second date, and he's remotely sensible, he'll simply tell you the truth, and you can move from thinking his mobile phone fell down a drain that he then heroically unscrewed with his teeth in a desperate bid to save your number. Or, he'll be a namby-pamby git unable to tell it like it is and will ask you out a second time (which clearly you will only

---

59 Forgive me if anyone out there still believes in the Second Coming, but really, why bother about the Second when it remains dubious whether the First actually happened?

accept if you liked him, as the idea isn't that everything should revolve around how he feels about you. Nor should you be seeking his approval).

Myth Five
Forsooth, thou shalt not taste of the forbidden fruit,
OR, MARRIED AND ATTACHED MEN ARE OUT OF BOUNDS

Most authors on the subject of dating are afraid to admit that falling in love is much like your relationship with your parents: you cannot choose who it happens with. Instead, these blinkered boobs don rose-tinted spectacles and opine that all relationships should be as pure as the driven snow and that you are a cheating, no-good whore if you end up dating, becoming infatuated with, or even sleeping with, a married or attached man. Yes, clearly it's dishonest, clearly there may be trust issues if you ever did get together with him, for what goes – and indeed sleeps – around comes around, and clear as the clearest, most tranquil, Caribbean sea, you have the morals of an alley cat if you help someone cheat on their wife. And yet … and yet, in a world where two in three marriages end in divorce, in a world where we have the freedom to live independent lives when we are married, in a world, in short, where a recent survey[60] shows that 14.6 per cent of men and 9.0 per cent of women have had overlapping sexual relationships in the last year, it's sad but true, you would hardly be at the top of the immorality pile if you date a married man.[61] End of sermon.

Myth Six
Abandon hope all ye whose fair knight useth not
the word boyfriend,
OR, IF HE IS UNCOMFORTABLE CALLING YOU HIS GIRLFRIEND
HE DOESN'T WANT TO TAKE THINGS ANY FURTHER

Remind me. Am I writing this in quill and ink or on my ultra modern laptop? The latter, dearies, the latter. Aren't we living in a time when

60 Source: One Plus One Marriage & Partnership Research.
61 But if you don't mind, please try not to date or sleep with my married man!

we can just let things flow? It's not as if the boyfriend police are going to bang on your door because he maintains you are just 'seeing each other', is it? If he hasn't mentioned the word yet, and you are hanging out in the traditional manner of boyfriend and girlfriend (namely, you are having an exclusive sexual relationship), it would be wrong to assume he doesn't like you – maybe he just wants to take things slowly. And after all, the slushiest story of all time itself says: 'What's in a name? A rose by any other name would smell as sweet …' and if Juliet can put up with it, then so can you! And hey, girlfriend, if him calling you 'girlfriend' means so much to you, you might want to have a word with yourself about why you are putting so much emphasis on it. Could it be you're not that into him and want an excuse to bail, but haven't got the nerve, or are you too afraid of being alone?

Myth Seven

In ye olde worlde of dating, thine knight shall ne'er be the one to take things too fast,
OR, HE'LL NEVER BE THE ONE TO FALL HEAD FIRST … FIRST

It's often said that it's always the woman who gets carried away with her emotions at the start of a relationship, but there's nothing stopping a guy getting it bad no sooner than he's laid eyes, hands, or whatever, on us too. This can be very confusing if you are used to stand-offish men who keep both feet on the ground when you first meet, and if we continue the footy talk, who seem like they'll never fall at your feet in adoration. A word of warning here: just as we should try not to rush into anything with our own emotions, we should seriously question the motives of a guy who seems to fall for us so quickly. Consider a friend of mine, who started dating a male friend after they had both experienced serious break-ups. Within weeks, he declared his undying love for her, and even though at first she viewed it only as a bit of fun, she got caught up in his enthusiasm and ended up falling for him hook, line and sinker. The day after she told him she loved him back, he got, you guessed it, cold feet!

I hope we've now put paid to a few of the dating myths of old and told it like it is in the real world of dating today. Now, if this means you might be tempted never to have anything more than a light-hearted look at another dating guide again, then so much the better. Another bonus would be if you've experienced 'menlightenment', that is, that you have resolved to make your dating decisions based on what *you* want, not based on what you think might be expected of you by your date, society or anyone else!

'That's all very well,' you might say, 'I'm feeling "menlightened" and you've covered the emotional side of things, but what about the really juicy stuff that happens when I'm single?' Fear not, my dating damsels in distress! The entire next chapter is dedicated to sex and the single girl – a time to take liberties as well as precautions, and for a shag-fest of truly shameless, yet blameless, behaviour.

Modern Dilemma

Dear Modern Maiden,

I have a confession. I'm a single woman who doesn't want a boyfriend. Not so shocking, is it? But the way some of my friends have reacted, you'd think I'd just confessed to raping tiny fluffy kittens with a foot-long dildo. I'm not married to my career, I don't have an ersatz companion in the form of a stinky pet, and nor do I conform to any other single female stereotype – I'm simply happy on my own and not looking to settle down with a significant other in the near future. Why, then, do my coupled-up friends continually try to match-make on my behalf? One even went as far as putting my name on a singles dating website, and since then, my email inbox has been clogged up with messages from weirdos, wasters and wankers. How can I persuade my friends to let me live a single life in peace?

Yours happily single,

Abby

Dear Abby,

Forget all that stuff about them living their single lives vicariously through you: most coupled-up bores genuinely believe they are doing you a favour, rescuing you from the horrors of singledom. I suggest you put an entry online for the friend who did the same to you, and give her a taste of her own medicine. Then maybe she'll understand that you have about as much desire as she does to be dating. This said, being single doesn't mean you have to lock yourself out of view, like some fragile, priceless masterpiece. Dusting yourself off every now and then and putting on the war paint will make the road to dating easier when you are ready to put yourself on view to the general public again!

Yours happily not-single,

MM

CHAPTER THIRTEEN
Sex and the Single Girl:
Sex without Love

When we gals indulge that pubescent impulse to don the shortest skirt imaginable, push our boobs up and out as far as possible (more often than not with the aid of cotton wool or a push-up bra), and bat our eyelashes with a come-hither look at every passing male (in short, whenever we express our sexuality), we don't half get it in the neck, from society in general and the media alike. For proof, just steal a glance at the headlines in any daily newspaper: 'Young women have the highest number of sexual partners ever.' Gasp! 'Boozy floozies are having sex and waking up the next day with no memory of it.' Shock! 'Teenage girls are losing their virginity at an ever younger age.' Horror! Such moral panics conveniently forget that in other cultures, and indeed in our own for most of human history, young women are, or were, married off at the tender age of thirteen as soon as they were physically able to conceive children. Nowadays, after fifty years of sexual liberation, we are berated if we show an inkling of desire – or indeed thigh – and young women (and men) are encouraged in the US, and to a lesser extent in Europe, to vow pledges of virginity as part of promoting abstinence before marriage.

Thankfully, and as if we needed it, there is scientific evidence to show that the human female being naturally chaste is a load of balls. And I mean literally a load of balls. Because apparently we can tell by the size of the male's testicles how promiscuous the female of a species will be: the bigger the male's testes, the more sperm is produced, and it's implied the more females there are vying for his attention. Human males, by primate standards, have middle-of-the-range testicles, which mean that we human ladies are rather less monogamously inclined than we have been led to believe.[62] Or to put it more crudely, scientists have 'discovered' that women like a bit of slap and tickle as much as the next fella. And what's more, it's entirely natural! This will come as no surprise to the majority of you wanton women out there, although as this theory proves, there is nothing wanton about wantin' to get your oats every now and then.

It's all very well when we are attached and sex is available at the drop of a hat (or knickers), but where does that leave us between the sheets when we are between men? The modern single woman basically has three options when it comes to sex: the one-night stand, casual sex with an acquaintance or friend, or self-gratification.[63] In this chapter we'll take a sneaky peek at these amour-less activities and how we can survive in times of sex without love!

ONE-NIGHT STANDS

There are two schools of thought on the one-night stand – either they are miserable encounters carried out by the depraved and the needy, or they are the physical manifestation of women's sexual liberation. Either way, it is oft cited that one-night stands cannot possibly leave a woman 'fulfilled'. Let's not skirt around the issue, because what's being implied here is that women cannot be sexually satisfied (that is achieve the 'big O') by a one-night fling, given that some find it hard enough to climax with their significant other. This is to ignore the fact that, orgasm or not, one-night stands can be delicious sexual adventures of derring-do! In fact, while we are on the subject, let's compare the one-night stand to an expedition by a brave explorer: there is the trepidation at encountering the unknown, the element of danger, and we come back having discovered something about ourselves, although hopefully not having picked up any nasty diseases from visiting foreign 'parts'! As every

62 *The Observer*, 3 September 2000.
63 Or four if you count celibacy, a viable option for those who need an interval from intercourse, but I don't think you need any tips from me on how to do, or rather, not do it!

explorer worth their salt should know, the key to a successful expedition is all in the preparation, and as such, here is the low-down on getting your pants down on your sexual voyage of discovery.

The mission

To get laid, of course. And well. What you are both after is sexual gratification, but there is an unwritten rule that any – shall we call them sexual foibles – should be left out of the bedroom for these briefest of encounters. So, if the only way you can get off is by wearing crotchless woolly knickers and shouting 'tally-ho', whilst beating his bum with a riding crop, you are probably better off trying to meet people through specialist dating agencies. Similarly you don't expect him to plead 'sit on my face' as soon as you hit the sack, and spend your short time together trying to bore all the way to Australia through your vagina with his tongue.[64] As this will be the most fleeting of flirtations, the onus – or anus if you will – is on you to let him know which is your orifice, position and style of preference, in order to make the most of your liaison dangereuse. Don't be afraid to speak up. He'll enjoy it if you do!

The equipment

Every good Girl Guide knows that one should always be prepared in order for any expedition to go without a hitch. Since you cannot predict when your next romantic flash in the pan(ties) will be, your handbag should always be well equipped with the following.

🌸 Condoms of all shapes, sizes and varieties. The last thing you need is your fella claiming he is so big that condoms are uncomfortable – in which case, lucky you – or that they tend to slip off his small, but perfectly formed, penis – in which case, let's hope his talents lie elsewhere. Numerous sex guides and dating manuals will proffer

---

64 And if you are reading this in Australia, Europe or the US.

elaborate techniques of rolling on a condom with your tongue in order to make the 'task' of wearing one more appealing for him. But here's a novel way of making sure he does: tell him he ain't getting any unless he dons the latest fashion in latex, tout de suite. That'll soon have him rolling one on with vim and vigour!

* (S)extras should be kept to a minimum. Okay, it is possible to have a discreet stash of lubricant, as many brands are now available in handy portable sachets (including the fun heat-and-tingle varieties), but keeping a stock of vibrators or dildos is not advisable lest your handbag spills open at work/on your mother's kitchen table/on the Tube as you root around for a mint.

* Drink and drugs are not so much an accessory as an integral part of the evening for some. The trick here is to consume enough to lose your inhibitions but not so much that you lose your sense of safety or indeed your dignity. Remember, laddy-like but ladylike at all times!

* Supposedly 'modern' etiquette guides suggest you squirrel away a clean pair of knickers in the darkest echelons of your handbag, in case you end up staying over somewhere other than base camp (your home). But the Modern Maiden knows it is more important to keep a few essential grooming items to keep you fresh and vaguely human-looking the next day (perfume, eye make-up remover, eyelash curlers and other such lifesavers you're unlikely to find in a boy's bathroom). Let's face it, you probably won't have been wearing your knickers long anyway, and if worse comes to worst, you can always turn them inside out. Certainly it's more likely your fellow passengers on the bus to work would notice your panda eyes or if you smelled, than if you were wearing yesterday's undergarments!

The pitfalls

Every awesome adventure has its dangers and the one-night stand is no exception. We were taught Stranger Danger from a young age, so we ought to recognise that there is an element of risk, riding off into the sunset (or to the deepest darkest suburbs on a stinky night bus) with a guy whose name you've not quite caught. However, in these days of mobile phones there is no excuse not to send a quick text to your best mate/flatmate and give them your co-ordinates and his name (if you can bear to ask for it yet again). To avoid such complications, it usually makes sense to bring him back to base camp (your place) so you have more control over the situation.

Other setbacks are of a more physical nature – for instance, if unfairly he can't get firm because of too much alcohol or drugs and your adventure becomes mission(ary) position impossible! The key thing here is not to panic. Continue with kissing and cuddling for half an hour and try not to bring attention to the 'little problem' as it will only exacerbate it. If after this time and a strong cup of coffee he is still floppier than J Lo's last movie release, then make it clear you expect your needs to be served by other means. After all, you went into this as a sort of deal, didn't you, and you don't expect to be short-changed due to his, ahem, 'shortcomings'?

The debrief

The morning after the night before can be one of life's more embarrassing moments. They don't call the bandy-legged trudge to the bus stop or train station in yesterday's clothes The Walk Of Shame for nothing. Here, more than anywhere, the Modern Maiden's mantra of 'shameless, yet blameless' has resonance. If you are in base camp, so much the better, as you can invent an important meeting or task that gives you an excuse to boot him out; what's more, the only walk of shame will be the trip to the kitchen past your flatmates while you make him a cup of tea (or strong coffee, see above). If you are at his place, gather your thoughts and your possessions and thank him politely for a lovely evening, making sure you leave before you've been asked to do so. At this point, you need to consider if you want it to be an Oh! Oh! Oh! revoir rather than a simple goodbye. You should only ask for his number if he's hot to trot; otherwise, let sleeping dogs lie and move on to your next perfunctory paramour! If not, the major pitfall of such a rapid romance could rear its ugly head … feeling rejected and/or becoming emotionally involved. If you are unable to detach yourself from the emotional side of things, perhaps you should skip this section and fly solo for a little while (see below for a 'handful' of masturbation tips).

Remember that your mates may also want to take part in the debrief, and will inevitably ask you to dish the dirty details on your shady shenanigans the next day. The rule here is never to cuss and tell: if he didn't live up to sexpectations, you can hardly blame him for trying, can you, you irresistible wench? And you never know – even if it was a bumpy ride, there may be a time when you consider giving him another road test!

CASUAL SEX AND FUCK BUDDIES

The term 'fuck buddy' is swiftly becoming part of the modern vernacular, but for those of you who have not yet come across this crude new coinage, allow me to explain: a fuck buddy is someone with whom you share no strings, emotions or inhibition-attached sex, on the mutual understanding that you want sex and nothing more, and is a – sexily-stockinged – step up in the commitment stakes from the one-night stand. Well, so far as your commitment extends to agreeing to meet once in a while for a good old-fashioned romp. A positive feature of having a fuck buddy is that the sex should always be good (as clearly you'd be bonkers not to choose someone, um, bonkable for the role). But remember, you are not acting out a tired male fantasy here of sex on tap, but instead, you should go with your own flow to find out what floats your boat, and any other watery idiom you care to mention! The other important defining feature is that you should both be single. It's no good being fuck buddy to a guy with a girlfriend … unless it's with her blessing.

This kind of liaison can be a good way to perfect your sexual repertoire. For, having established that the chemistry works but that you're not emotionally attached, you are free to let your imaginations, and your fingers, roam. And, in case your imaginations are taking a short vacation, here are some ideas of what you might like to try (or perfect if you have tried already).

* Sticking your finger up his bum in order to make him come harder (especially good when giving a blowie at the same time), seeing how much of a guy's balls you can fit in your mouth and whether humming while you do so makes him sing with pleasure, or wanking him under your armpit, in your cleavage (if you have one), or twixt your thighs. Anywhere and anything goes! Because what you are learning about the male anatomy now will stand you in good stead for any future love, who might not appreciate being used as a sexual guinea pig.[65]

* Making a brief foray into S & M or other kinky areas into which you would not normally dare venture, such as boning up (ha ha) on your spanky-panky skills and/or playing the dominatrix. But it's worth remembering that, while your fuck buddy may enjoy being trampled on in stiletto heels, you'll have to tread carefully, literally, with a future fella: one man's exquisite torture is another's well, simply, torture.

* Getting your tongue around … dirty talk. As some may find this a serious linguistic challenge, let's have a quick language lesson with examples of good and bad sex talk, for which the basic formula is: crude + ridiculous = good dirty talk, gynaecological + shyness = bad. But do remember dirty talk tastes can be very subjective. A 'throbbing member' may be arousing to some, and just bloody hilarious to others. Or if you're lucky – both! …

---

65 And if you are thinking of using an actual guinea pig as your fuck buddy, again I refer you to specialists who can perhaps offer you some help.

You want to say	Bad dirty talk	Good dirty talk
Give me oral sex.	Would you mind awfully, you know, going down there (said with a stammer and a blush).	Come and taste my cunt honey.
Shall we make love?	I am ready for penetration with your penis now. Please.	Pump me with your love muscle, you super sexy stud.
Take me in the bottom.	Would you mind awfully switching to my back passage?	Do me in my tight little bum hole. Oh, yeah.
I am having an orgasm.	Thank you darling, I'm gratified and reaching climax.	I'm coming, oh yes, I'm coming, big boy, fill me with your hot juice, I'm coming, oh yes, [ad infinitum] …
I want to give you oral sex.	[Clearly there is no bad way to tell a man you wish to give him a blow job.]	[Likewise, anything you say in this regard will sound good.]

- Perfecting your technique of asking for what you want in the sack. For instance, if he is playing a bit too rough, don't scream, 'What are you doing down there? You're breaking my precious love bud.' Simply try to distract him with some moves of your own, and if he's the opposite of rough and ready, practise having the balls to take the meek out of your geek.

- Doing it up the bottom: anal sex is a particularly good one to try with a fuck buddy because, as the saying goes, 'shit happens', or to put it another way, there is the possibility of leaky poo and squelchy noises. Yes, you trust him enough to do it, but you don't love him, so try not to give too much of a toss if either of these factors come into play! In order to avoid the grit-your-teeth-and-bare-it pain, use lots of lubricant and get him to start out by placing a few elegant fingers up your bottom first. The poo element should not be a problem, assuming you are sensible and don't scoff an entire vindaloo beforehand, and the squelch factor can be avoided with practise, and besides, who said sex wasn't meant to have some laughs?

The downside to having a fuck buddy is when one or other of you starts to want something more. If it's him and you're unsure whether to break ties, there is nothing to stop you going on a date to see how you get on in the more conventional world of dating. If it is you, and you are fairly sure the feelings aren't reciprocated, make an exit quick sharp before you get hurt. And you should certainly never do this thinking that it will 'bring someone round' to liking you in way that stretches beyond your agreed parameters (unless you are shit hot in the sack).

MASTURBATION

It is hard to get some women to own up to their onanism in the cold light of day, but as soon as the lights are dimmed you'll find them flicking off to a mucky book with their rampant rabbit set to 'multiple orgasm'. There is no excuse not to be well-practised in pleasuring yourself when single and you should take every opportunity to do so (although you don't want to end up with a habit, so on the bus/under your desk at work/at the swimming baths aren't valid options, my mas-turbatin' maidens!). Although I expect that you're all well (per)versed with your own techniques, here are a couple of suggestions you may not have thought of, in case the shine has come off usual finger, thumb and vibrator methods.

Shower

Why not use shower power and angle the stream of water from the showerhead at your clitoris, or vulva, if your clitoris is particularly sen-sitive? Of course, this only works to climactic effect if you have one of those modern power showers. You could be waiting longer for an orgasm than a eunuch in a harem if you have one of those daft plastic shower attachments, leading to major embarrassment when your flatmates start banging on the door wondering what's become of you.

Get your leg over

Experimenting with different positions is not just fun for couples, it can also add a new dimension to self-pleasuring if you are getting bored with your usual modus operandi. You can go 'on top', lie face down, and use the extra pressure on your hand to stimulate your clitoris. Or, why not try doggy style, using beads or a silk scarf to rub against your bits? All putting the fun back into looking after number one!

Foreign objects

Often the temptingly phallic curves of a hairbrush/broom handle/perfume bottle can seem like a good idea at the time, but remem-ber the vagina can have extremely strong suction powers at times of arousal, so it's better to find something that has a flared base to save an embarrassing trip to A & E (all very well if you had a lover by your side to titter with, but on your own, this experience would be every bit socially, as well as physically, painful).

We started out in this chapter asking how the single girl can cope with sex without love, but as Woody Allen famously put it, masturbation is sex with someone you love, so maybe there is hope after all! Joking aside, the point is how you get yours when you are single is nobody's business but your own, and you should not have to answer to anyone on the matter. So come on my sassy singletons, may the phwoars be with you!

But what to do when sex and love become entangled, and the first flushes of lust and yet more lust evolve into a relationship? In the next chapter, we'll consider what to do when taking things further, both emotionally and sexually, and when the time may be right to bring things to an end.

Modern Dilemma

Dear Modern Maiden,

I have been seeing a nice guy for a few weeks and, after several dates fumbling and fretting, we finally got around to doing the do last night. The sex was fine; he was very attentive and all, but there is one small problem. And I mean small. Or should I say tiny? I'm of course talking about his penis. Would it be deeply shallow of me not to agree to further dates, simply because he is challenged in the manhood department?

Yours frustratedly,

Polly

Dear Polly,

I am sorry you are at sixes and sevens. Or should that be at three and five … inches! Sorry. I don't mean to mock your dilemma, but what he lacks in the underpants, you seem to lack in depth. You say he's a nice guy and the sex was fine. What are you waiting for? A well-hung Norse god with the body of Adonis and the brain of Aristotle to descend from the heavens? You might do well to reflect that in many parts of Asia, the cultural norm is not to discuss small penises, but rather some women are said to have very big vaginas. Besides, back in the penis-centric West, the given view is that most penises are about the same size when erect, so unless you're planning a weekend at a nudist camp, I shouldn't worry too much about it. What I would say about your impending relationship, though, is that you may wish to aspire to more than just a 'nice guy' where the sex is 'fine'.

Yours without size mattering,

MM

Dear Modern Maiden,

I feel I have nowhere left to turn, so, since you seem to dole out advice with honesty, if not sincerity, I thought I would try you. The problem is, I lack confidence when sucking a man off, and I am sure I have lost at least a couple of good prospective boyfriends simply because I shy away from 'going there'. Could it be these blokes are basing their opinion of me based on my performance (or lack of it) in the sack?

Yours shyly,

Tessa

Dear Tongue-Tied Tessa,

I could flick through a million sex books and come up with all sorts of advice to make him come with a flick of your tongue: from suck, don't blow, to wetter is better, to anything goes, the list for getting the measure of his pleasure is endless. But how about this, for a modern take on such advice: anything you try will be met with rapturous thanks, and if you really don't enjoy doing it, don't? But that wasn't really your question, was it? Dunno whether these particular blokes have not wanted to take things further because you don't want to take their things in your mouth, but try not to let it become an obsession. Why not try your technique on someone you're not that into instead? Who knows, maybe that's what the dumpers were doing on you, and felt they weren't up to it themselves?

Yours suggestively,

MM

CHAPTER FOURTEEN
Taking It Further:
How to Begin (and End) a Relationship

We are obsessed by firsts: we gasp at feats of human endeavour, churning out reams of nostalgia devoted to the first man to walk on the moon or climb Everest; we wonder at the sporting achievements of record-breaking athletes, counting down as the 100m sprint is run in ever-fewer seconds; and we gawp in ghoulish amazement at breakthroughs in modern science, such as the world's first face transplant. In our private lives, firsts also have special significance. Most parents drool sentimentally at the thought of their baby's first word, steps or smile[66] and we all remember (fondly or not) our first day at school, at university/college, in our first 'proper' job. It's these milestones that help us understand where we are in life, and this is true most of all in our sex lives, where perhaps our most evocative life firsts occur, our 'first date' and 'first time'.

When a relationship is over and we think back on it, it is the firsts and lasts that stick in our mind, the in-between bit somehow getting forgotten in a dreamy haze of fond memories over the beginning and a nightmarish cloud of recriminations over the end. Just think of all the love songs you know about falling in love and breaking up; there aren't many to the tune of 'the sex was still okay, pom-de-pom, we were getting along nicely, be-wop-a-doo-wop, but we sometimes argued about whose turn it was to do the washing up, la-la-la'. For this reason, in this chapter devoted to sexual and romantic relationships we will dwell nostalgically on firsts, mooch self-indulgently over the 'lasts'

---

66 The last often wrongly, I may add, as at three weeks old your baby isn't happily giving you a gummy grin; rather, it's probably suffering from wind.

(the dumpings), and take a necessary detour to think about the in-betweeny bit: the relationship itself.

FIRSTS

In the modern world, when your knickers have often been whipped off before you've even had a five-minute conversation, nine times out of ten you've already 'taken things further' before your relationship has begun. How then, in these care- and knicker-free days, to define the moment when you are 'going steady', or he becomes your 'main squeeze'? If we use relationship firsts as our benchmark, we certainly cannot count on first kisses, or even the first time you make love, as an indication that things are moving onto the next level, and that you like one another enough to be 'boyfriend and girlfriend'.[67] The following firsts, and tips on how to get through them, will provide a more contemporary barometer on your relationship's outlook and whether things are hotting up. (Please note that if it's him who's instigated the first couple on the list, it's a sure-fire sign he is burning for commitment.)

The first time you meet his mates

Essentially the problem with meeting his mates is that you want them to like you, but not so much that they want to fuck you. Moreover, you want to like them but you don't want to want to fuck them, either. Or at least if you do want to fuck them, you should certainly make sure neither they, nor your boyfriend, notice. Flirting is therefore not a sensible option to win them over, but then again, neither is pretending to be one of the lads and downing so many pints that you forget you're not meant to be flirting! (Laddy-like, yet ladylike will have his mates eating out your hand.) Here I am talking about meeting the males in his tribe, but meeting any female friends will be an entirely different and altogether more dangerous prospect. They will be as protective of their

67 See Chapter Twelve about setting too much store on this in any case.

pal as a mother hen around her chicks, and you will be very wise not to ruffle their feathers! If you are lucky they will treat you with the some respect, but remember: they got there first, so don't be too surprised if they don't.

The first time you meet his family

Many dating and relationship guides put meeting friends and family in the same category. Piffle. Ingratiating yourself with his family is a lot more complex, as you have to subtly appear at once maternal (father and mother may both be pining after grandkids), pretty with a slutty undertone (father will be much friendlier if you are and you'll need him onside to deal with the matriarch), generous (his mother will want to share him with you, but don't worry, your portion will get bigger over time), and many other things, depending on whether they are a traditional or modern family. It therefore pays to ask questions before you get together so that you don't rock up in your 'Jesus Was a Black Man' t-shirt only to discover they're Born-Again Christians, or screech to a halt outside the door of their solar powered eco-friendly home in your gas-guzzlin' SUV. Yes, you can slowly reveal your true identity but only once you've met them a few times and feel something like a glow of warmth in the relationship.

The first time you don't make any effort

At the same time that you stop wearing lip-gloss or having your hair done each time you meet, so the gloss might be wearing off the first flushes of romance in your relationship. For there will certainly come a time when you are happy to answer his knock at the door in your pyjamas because it's late, you'd just stepped out the shower when he called round, and you can't be bothered to get dressed up. Do be careful, mind, when letting him know you are in the comfort zone, and you are probably still better off answering the door in your sexiest (clean) pyjamas, or nothing, rather than a mouldy old nightdress with yoghurt stains down the front. Sluttish, not slovenly, will keep him on his toes and in your bed!

The first argument

The first argument can be a good sign in your relationship. No, really! This simply means you are both no longer on your guard, pussy-footing around one another and certain issues. Mind you, it can come as quite a shock if your first few weeks or months together have been as genteel as a ladies' knitting circle, both of you well-mannered and on your best behaviour, only for life to become as tense and nasty as a no-holds-barred court case as soon as you have your first few cross words. Allegations may fly about, with your boyfriend playing the belligerent barrister, while you, his cowering girlfriend, stand accused of 'air-headedness in the first degree' or any similar minor crime or misdemeanour. Or maybe it's you who has brought the case to court and he sullenly pleads the Fifth Amendment,[68] stonewalling you or saying nothing at all. Either way, if your arguing styles vary drastically, it won't be possible to argue effectively, and both of you will need to give in a little or you can give up the ghost on any hope of reaching a conclusion! It will be worth compromising, for as soon as you are reconciled, you will be able to kiss and make up or rather kiss and make out, which will make the argument seem worth it in the first place. Well, almost.

The first time you let ... shall we say ... loose

So, we've gone through a few firsts that are clear indications for the contemporary chick that your relationship has stepped up a gear, but

68 Even if you live outside of the US he can use this excuse; it's a fictional argument I'm talking about here, after all!

there is one final, more difficult, relationship benchmark that I am sure most ladies have been relieved to reach in more ways than one. This is when you can spend a night in his bed without tossing and turning, writhing in pain with a crippling bellyache, from holding in either a poo or trapped wind, because you don't want to him to know that you have unpleasant bodily functions just like everybody else. Yes, the real first to watch out for is the moment when you pop out a little fart and can simply turn to him with a smile and say 'whoops' rather than wanting to curl up and die the slowest, most miserable death possible, or perhaps the first time you visit his bathroom without spending an hour squirting his deodorant and waiting for any lingering smells to dissipate! Strange as it may seem, these messy moments may let you know you are totally at ease with him and trust him enough to take things further!

THE IN-BETWEEN BIT OR THE RELATIONSHIP ITSELF

However, life being the bitch that it is, it's just when you've taken this smug step toward 'we' instead of 'me' that often one or other, or even both of you, starts to suffer from cold feet. Because as much as you may have pined after having that special someone in your life, you may soon discover that life à deux is not all it's cracked up to be, especially if your boyfriend's irritating little habits start to drive you crackers or you discover he has a love of crack. Maybe the little 'Post-it' love notes he used to leave on the fridge have started woefully curling just like the mouldy bag of lettuce inside, or maybe he only sends you flowers after a quarrel or when a relative dies, both signs that he has become complacent and is taking you for granted. Now could be the make or break time in the relationship, and you may decide he needs a kick up the bum at boyfriend boot camp. At this (to date) imaginary camp[69] he will learn that he'd better shape up or ship out unless he learns to

69 Although I am sure it won't be long before some dude makes this imaginary camp into a reality TV show. Royalties please!

deliver on the three relationship Rs required to keep you enamoured of him: respect, romance and, err, let me think of something else beginning with r – rumpy-pumpy? He won't be allowed back in to your life until he has learned by heart the following boyfriend drill call, to be practised each and every morning in front of you, his very own Sergeant Major, or rather, Mistress (in person or if you don't live together, over the 'phone).

1 I will continue to wine, dine and 69 my girlfriend even after the honeymoon period has ended. Ma'am, yes, Ma'am!

2 In an age of diaries, palm pilots, blackberries and plain old-fashioned memory, I will not forget dates/birthdays/to leave out the rubbish. Ma'am, yes, Ma'am!

3 I will keep my private porn collection, just that, private. I realise that it is plainly not romantic to find a jazz mag or a man-size box of tissues by your side of the bed during one of our mid-week trysts. Ma'am, yes, Ma'am!

4 I will not wince at any talk of settling down/future plans/weekend breaks or foreign holidays. I appreciate that with my 29th birthday around the corner this does not seem very grown up. Ma'am, yes, Ma'am!

5 I will, in short, make every effort to be thoughtful, romantic and kind, if you promise to do the same. Ma'am, yes, Ma'am!

PUTTING UP WITH HIM NOW YOU'RE, ERM, PUTTING HIM UP

Having passed the boyfriend boot camp test, your minds may wander to stepping things up a notch, and moving in together. A knotty subject if ever there was one, a biggie in the commitment stakes to be sure, and maybe one or both of you is putting it off longer than your next visit to the dentist. Perhaps the following Modern Maiden's 'Are you ready-to-move-in?' checklist can help, and will have you dreaming of domestic bliss, or possibly give you reservations about co-habitation.

1 His mother has started calling him at your place/your mother calls you at his place.

2 You are both financially solvent and can pay your own way.

3 It is do or die time as one of you has been offered a job in another city.

4 You share the same taste in soft furnishings (believe me, nothing can kill romance dead quicker than a man's love of brown and orange in a pair of curtains).

5 You are such a pair of loved-up saddos that you've dropped all your other friends.

6 You are prepared (or he is, if you would be moving into his place) to clear more space for his possessions than a single drawer. And the cutlery drawer at that.

7 You are pregnant (and keeping it).

8 Your flatmates call the police when they find you sitting at the breakfast table: they'd forgotten you exist.

If you can tick off three or more from the above list, perhaps it's a sign you are both up for moving in. If you can't, and you're still daydreaming about picking out brown and orange curtains, we could read into it that you keener than him to set up home together. You should never take this to mean that he wants to break off with you, but just that he wants to take things slowly. Don't worry too much, as this is a point of negotiation you can come back to in six months. In the meantime, you'd be advised to enjoy the plus points of living apart from him, as once moved in, you may sadly miss the halcyon days of clearing up after one person, paying your own bills and having the bathroom to yourself, as you would never have imagined. Domesticity can be every bit as boring as it sounds and you should be prepared for mundanity as well as the obvious pleasure of waking up next to one another every day. It could also involve a lot more work for you. It has been best explained by Jerry Hall's famous quote: 'My mother said it was simple to keep a man: you must be a maid in the living room, a cook in the kitchen and a whore in the bedroom.'

Despite the quaint last century-ness of this statement, she may sadly have a point about men's expectations of cohabitation. If you can afford it, and it's not against your principles, having a cleaner may stop any possible domestic disputes over the chores (as we talked about in greater detail in Chapter Eight).

KEEPING THE LUST ALIVE

As for the whore in the bedroom, well, all relationships have their ups and downs, which to put it crudely can affect the old in-out, in-out, and it's fairly inevitable that your five-times-a-night romps of old will soon fizzle out into five times a week/month/year depending on your age/stamina/sex-drive. Here is a subtle updating of the ubiquitous sexpertise you find in magazines or sex manuals on how to relight the fire with your beloved, or rather how the Modern Maiden can put the stud back into her bedroom dud.

* Forget absence makes the heart grow fonder; abstinence makes the cock grow harder. Simply refuse your favours three times in a row and he'll soon be begging for it. Although if this makes him lose interest altogether, you may have to change tack.

* And do something deliberately tacky, like shaving your minky and sending him a Polaroid of it with a naughty note of your dishonourable intentions. (Send it to his home address where you can subsequently destroy it, not to his place of work, or by email, as I am not in favour of 'private' shots becoming public property!)

* Have it off with someone else or pretend that you are. Not that I'm a cheerleader for infidelity or lying, but if it is lack of sex that worries you, research shows that when one partner is having an affair, the sex life with their legitimate partner may get a boost. And if you tell him you're having an affair, maybe jealousy will make him pull his finger out – or rather put it in. (The latter only to be tried if you are sure he won't dump you, natch!)

* Fantasise. If you are going through the motions of your usual routine (he fingers you for what seems like an eternity but is in fact five minutes, you hump for another ten in one of three favoured positions), there's nothing like an illicit romp with Brad Pitt/Daffy

Duck/the milkman, or whoever else gets your juices flowing, to see you through it. And don't worry if your randy reveries seem to stretch beyond the realms of normality. Nancy Friday has devoted entire books to women's fantasies[70] that may put you at ease about the bizarre qualities of your own RomCom-esque romps or bestial bonks, depending.

● Finally, if it's you that's finding sex a chore, think of novel ways to make him come to get things over with quicker, for instance by giving an impromptu slutty performance, fingering yourself while talking dirty (see previous chapter for dirty talk tips) and encouraging him to touch himself up. This way if you're finding him less than attractive, he won't even have to get his grubby mitts on you. Watch out for that flying jism though!

LASTS

If you are still malcontent after sending him to boyfriend boot camp, moving in together, or trying to put the necessary bit back into your sex life (i.e. the sex!), it might be time to come to terms with the fact that every relationship has a shelf life, some more perishable than others, and, if you'll indulge me, I'd like to develop this thought further: the passion junkies among you will tend to shorter romances, like double cream perhaps, seductively sweet at first but which soon curdle or turn sour. Then we have something a bit steadier, a partnership more akin to a starchy carbohydrate (such as pasta or bread) that we crave and find moreish, and can be jazzed up with other ingredients, but ultimately is too samey if you have it every day. I suppose that, if we are honest, what most of us are ultimately after is a relationship like that store cupboard saviour, the bottle of fine wine, that retains its fizz and sparkle and may even improve over time. But then again, sometimes the finest wine can become corked, and a successful long-term partnership can spoil.

70 For example, 'My Secret Garden: Women's Sexual Fantasies' (Quartet Books, 2001).

Now, many stuffy old relationship manuals will suggest different ways of keeping your man, and we gals may go all out to ensure he still likes us, by dressing to the nines, making him his favourite meals and showering him with compliments and gifts. And if these desperate measures fail, and he dumps us, we are told to maintain our dignity, to shy away from acts of revenge and basically not lose our cool. Come on, lasses! Isn't it time we reversed this antiquated advice and became 'menlightened' again, as in Chapter Twelve? Shouldn't we be mulling over whether we want to keep our man and ask ourselves whether we still like him, not worry about the reverse? Let us, as an antidote to this man-centric advice, resolve to dump the chump in our lives when his time comes, let's take the bitching out of ditching and instead put as much thought and sensitivity into breaking up as we do to into falling in love, and let's indulge our grief (in a grown-up way if possible) if some crazy fool has given us the elbow. Easier said than done, you may say, and as such, as a counterpoint to the namby-pamby advice said manuals usually churn out, the following recommendations should see you through the dark days of dumping, be you the dumper or the dumpee.

How to dump him

1 Never mind the Seven-Year Itch; I've met plenty of folks who get a Two-Year Twitch, which is that tendency for thoughts to drift toward infidelity or moving on when things have started to get a little dull (indeed, in this fast-paced day and age, anyone who gets to seven years before having these thoughts deserves a medal of honour!). Before scratching the itch or satisfying that twitch, you should consider carefully whether it's just a relationship cold snap, and if there's a chance that you may warm to him again. If you ditch him now, only to change your mind a month down the line, you may be shocked to find out that he's the one who's moved on.

2 One sign that he is more of a lame duck than a golden goose is if, for the past year, you have consulted everyone from your mother, to the milkman, to the local mystic and her crystal ball, as to your sweet-

heart's suitability. If even the latter is fed up with your dithering, it's definitely time to stop procrastinating and start eradicating!

3 Violence, habitual infidelity[71] and him putting you down (in private or in public) are all valid reasons for consigning him to the slag heap of the past.

4 A stingy Xmas present/saying 'Yes, your bum does look big in it … but I love you anyway'/wanting the occasional night off, are not. Sure we've talked about sending him to boyfriend boot camp if he becomes complacent, but what you can't expect is for everything in the garden, bedroom, bathroom, etc. to be rosy at all times. Perfectionism is a quality to be admired, but one best put to one side if you want something deeper than the relationship equivalent of a rock pool.

5 There are tales aplenty of modernity producing novel and selfish ways to dump, such as giving him the brush off by text/fax/email/Post-it note stuck on the fridge. All shameless methods, yes, but not particularly blameless. Of course, if he's acted like a total tosser and shagged your best mate, these processes of elimination are valid, but if it's been three years and you've fallen out of love, you owe him an explanation of sorts.

6 Often, when doing the dirty deed in person, platitudes and clichés are doled out with more frequency than alcopops at a hen night (aka bachelorette party for those of you over the Atlantic). The following exit lines provide a more honest approach to bidding him good riddance, while sparing his feelings from the cold, hard facts of your decision to dump.

71 This one's up to you and maybe you have an open relationship. If not, and he does the dirty on you more than once, I think we could safely say monogamy is not his strong point.

What You Are Thinking	Don't Say	Do Say
I don't fancy you any more, you big lump.	It's not you, it's me.	But dear, haven't you been saying you wanted to spend more time in the GYM [stressing this last word for full effect]?
I am in love with your best friend.	Something has come between us.	Don't worry. We'll still see lots of one another. I am sure we'll keep in touch … via Darren.
I can't go out with a guy who wears prettier knickers than me.	We're too similar for this to work.	Who will get to keep the posh panties collection?
I was deeply embarrassed when you brought a guitar to my birthday party and started singing in front of my friends.	I don't think we're singing from the same hymn sheet.	Have you thought about a career in busking?
I've been offered a job in Paris and have no intention of taking you with me.	We're in different places right now.	See ya! Wouldn't wanna be ya! [Who cares about his feelings? You'll be miles away!]

7 If he can't handle the rejection, he will probably fall into one of two categories of dumpees-in denial: the lovelorn cling-on or the scary stalker. The cling-on is a fairly harmless beast, sending you flowers and love letters, perhaps calling and texting at all hours with expressions of undying love. A healthy dose of sangfroid and matter-of-factness will turn him off quicker than responding emotively or dramatically (he will think you care), but do try to have a heart and consider his feelings. The stalker is not a force to be reasoned with. He may be angry and aggressive, and turn up at your place of work or home, demanding an explanation. Be cool with him too but certainly don't spare his feelings. And don't be shy about calling the cops if things get out of hand!

8 A last point on this matter. If you are feeling too cowardly to ditch him, it sometimes pays to bide your time if you think he is about to lay his cards on the table and show you the red card himself. After all, the person who's been chucked gets much more tea and sympathy than the one to do the chucking!

How to be dumped

1 In the fantastical world of dating books, we are not meant to express any emotion when we are dumped by someone we liked, lusted after, or even loved, and we are expected not to get hurt, lose our cool or get hung up on the bloke who has rejected us. Yeah, right. At the very time when we feel our most emotionally vulnerable and long to wallow self-indulgently in our grief, it is suggested we put a brave face on it. Not that we should become cling-ons or stalkers as above, but we will get over him so much quicker if we deal with things there and then. Why not, then, moon around so much that you nearly cause an eclipse, or cry so hard that you're mistaken for an escapee from the local zoo because of your smudgy panda eyes? You'll feel so much the better for it.

2 At the very time of writing scientists have discovered there aren't plenty more fish in the sea! Don't panic, though, as supplies should last another fifty years … so it's only your granddaughters who will need to worry. Possible ecological disasters aside, and I know this one's hard to take, with over six billion people on the planet, there is bound to be (if we stick to the fishy imagery) another 'catch' for you, and maybe this one will be the dish, if not of the day, but of your life.

3 Forget what supposedly modern etiquette and dating guides, and your common sense, tell you: deleting his number from your mobile phone, or if you are an old-fashioned gal, address book, serves no purpose whatsoever. Firstly, you will probably have it memorised anyway; secondly, what is the harm in drunken dialling and losing a little face? (The latter point has an expiry date of about a month after you break up, mind you.) He had the gall to reject you, and it shows more self-respect to give him a piece of your mind than disappearing into the back of beyond without so much as a harrumph!

4 Just as your possessions, if you have been living together, will need to be divvied up, so might your friends. And I don't mean threatening to split 'em in two à la Samson and Deliliah. As a rule of thumb, he can cherrypick from the friends he had BC (before coupledom) and vice-versa (although you might suggest he's welcome to any of yours he happens to have slept with). A little time AD (after 'divorce') you might start seeing his closest mates again, but not if you're only doing so as a way to get back into his good books (and pants!). On the other hand, good luck, my mischievous maidens, if you are trying to get into theirs!

In this chapter we reviewed what happens, for better and worse, when we take things further with our relationships and how we can make the most of them from beginning to end. And while we are on the subject of for better, for worse, the next chapter will deal with all things weddings, engagements and married life for those who are taking things the furthest step of all.

Modern Dilemma

Dear Modern Maiden,

I'm enraged as my boyfriend just broke up with me because he caught me snogging someone behind a pillar in our favourite Saturday night hang-out. Thing is, that someone was a lady, and as I keep telling him, that shouldn't count. I thought all men liked watching a cheeky dose of girl-on-girl?

Yours angrily,

Anna

Dear Furious Bi-curious,

It's refreshing to hear some commonsense. From your boyfriend, I mean. If you had agreed to a monogamous relationship, you should stick to that agreement, which means you can't do the dirty on him with man, woman or beast. Mind you, a snog is not the worst of transgressions, so maybe you can sweet-talk him back into your life if you promise not to do it again. Of course, first having a word with yourself whether it really is a boy you're after. If not, I hope you had the common sense (if not decency) to get your lady-friend's number.

Yours sapphically,

MM

CHAPTER FIFTEEN
Wedded Bliss –
a Piece of Piss?

Perhaps it was, in a bolt from the blue, when your boyfriend got down on one knee, or maybe you took the initiative, as let's not forget there's nothing stopping you from popping the question nowadays. Whatever. You're now engaged to be married and are excitedly planning your wedding and life ahead together. But hold on a matrimonial minute! Is this truly what the Modern Maiden aspires to, gives in – or even just drifts in – to, in full knowledge that for years women have been oppressed, repressed and sometimes depressed by marriage and its 'duties'? Shouldn't we listen to the pro-feminists, who argue that weddings are an old-fashioned patriarchal trap with outrageously misogynistic traditions? Well, despite sounding like a bunch of long-winded party-poopers, they might have a point! And we're not just talking about the ridiculous notion of the father of the bride 'giving' her away as though she were his property. For we only have to scratch the surface to see that other traditions we soppily follow, caught up in the romance of it all, are altogether more sinister: the charming veil, which we think adds mystery to the proceedings, for example, some say dates back from a time when men simply threw a blanket over the woman of his choice and carried her off for a round of non-consensual jiggery-pokery,[72] or the true meaning of the cutting of the wedding cake, originally done by the bride alone, which signified her impending loss of virginity (she then handed out cake to the assembled guests to give them a share of her youthful fertility. Talk about everyone getting a piece of the action!).

72 This sounds like a load of codswallop to me, though, so don't be too alarmed.

Of course, there is no law that states that you must include these customs in your wedding ceremony, and these days, you could get married bungee jumping naked save for matching merkins, for all anybody cares (although your horrified family and friends may beg to differ). So the argument not to marry simply because of outdated patriarchal traditions just doesn't cut the mustard. That's not to say that further, better arguments not to marry don't fall out of the sky like confetti: many people are simply 'happy as they are', and you can't say fairer than that. Others can't live as man and wife even if they wanted to (preferring to live as man and man or wife and wife) and have to make do with civil partnerships instead. And yet still more people of all sexual predilections would rather walk down a central reservation than endure all the flamboyance and fuss of walking down the aisle. Then, last but not least, there is the small matter of divorce. Why, some might ask, if two out of three marriages end up down the toilet, should we take the plunge?

Well, the above arguments, and the bad press marriage gets, draw a (albeit prettily sequined) veil over the fact that many of us simply can't get enough of it. This could be seen as evidence of our entirely human, eternal optimism, that we think ours will be the one of the three marriages that lasts. Alternatively, it might just show our ever-growing love of consumerism, and that we like any excuse for a good shindig and to get dressed up nice and pretty! Whatever your motivation, there is no doubt that the road to marriage can be a rocky one,[73] and as such I have devised an 'I dos' and 'I don'ts' guide to this nerve-racking pre-nuptial period.

I dos

❈ Remember, first and foremost, that there are two of you getting married and don't obsess about how it is just *your* 'big day'. Amazingly enough, the groom may want to have some say in the

---

73 Although clearly the other kind of rocks we receive before the wedding are a positive point, not a negative one!

proceedings, so be prepared to adjust your expectations in the general direction of his. While you dream of a big white wedding, he may be thinking of a ceremony without the, erm, ceremony. Be prepared to compromise!

* Make a considered decision about names. No man should see it as an insult if you want to keep your family name, which may be as much a part of your identity as your right arm. In fact, there's nothing to stop him taking yours or even making a new one up together! Okay, it's a tradition for you to take on his moniker and you may have dreamed of doing so, doodling it on notebooks just to see how it looked (you saddo! Please remind yourself you're not five), but as we've seen earlier in the chapter, many other marital traditions have been consigned to the dustbin of history and the world did not fall off its axis.

* Try to find time to take (discreet) notes on what goes wrong during the pre-wedding build up, for inevitably something will. (For example, if you get stiffed on the cost of the flowers.) Because as we've seen, with many marriages failing, and second marriages on the up, you never know when the information may prove useful again!

I don'ts

* Avoid having a hen night/bachelorette party at an expensive spa resort or in a foreign city unless you are willing to pay for your hens, or you are all stinking rich. I know you are going to be Queen of the World for a day, but that doesn't mean you can expect your long-suffering friends to act like Ladies-in-Waiting, attending to your every whim. (Or they may become ladies waiting for you to bugger off and make new friends!)

* Refrain from (matri)moaning if someone asks if they can go 'off list' when buying a wedding present (apparently in some circles, this is considered a worse faux pas than attending the wedding in full bridal gown and tiara – and I mean if you're not the bride). Take it as a compliment that someone feels they know you well enough to

get you a truly personal gift. Or alternatively, take it as proof that they hate your guts (just as you suspected all these years), not least when they turn up with a 'unique' porcelain statuette of woodland faeries sharing a precious moment.

❀ Steer clear of worrying too much about any nagging doubts regarding your future life with your betrothed. Even the most loved-up of couples have these torturous, anxiety-ridden moments just before the ceremony. And who can blame them? Think about it logically, promising to remain monogamous for the rest of your born days is asking a lot of any human being.[74] (That wasn't very helpful, was it, my blushing brides-to-be?)

❀ Do not freak out if getting hitched doesn't go without a hitch! Perfect days only exist in fairytales, but so do nasty seven-headed, fire-breathing monsters, and they won't be on the guest list, will they? Try taking the day in your stride and you will enjoy it a whole lot more!

WEDDED BLISS – A PIECE OF PISS?

You've done it, and the stressful part is over! Or so you'd think. Because never mind the rules of engagement; when it comes to the battle of the sexes, it's the rules of marriage that matter in the end. And by this, I don't mean picking up your *Rules Book* again, for if the advice therein was bonkers before, when it comes to marriage it goes even further off the rails. Why not, it is suggested, 'act' independent by being busy, spending time with family and friends to keep your husband interested? Now, it's not that I am, in turn, suggesting you should ditch your bitches now that you've got a ring on your finger. Au contraire! It's that 'act' independent that smells fishy to me, as if this doesn't come naturally to the 21st-century wife. Worse still in this loopy list of marital *Rules*, is the advice that you may have to 'act single' in order to keep your spouse

---

74 We are a naturally promiscuous bunch, as I have suggested in previous chapters!

enamoured. Holy Matrimony, Batman! Surely we get married because we are secure, because we're sure we have made the right choice, and we don't have to play games anymore.

Nonetheless, it may make sense to set a few ground rules of your own in the turf war that is marriage – indeed, the first year can be notoriously difficult as you stalk about like cats marking out your territory (without the weeing on the floor, one hopes, although you never know with men, eh?). Now, your humble author wouldn't presume to suggest what these rules should be, each marriage being a precious flower that needs varying degrees of watering, pruning and plucking (or if you are very unlucky, a poisonous weed that should be put out of its misery *tout de suite*!). One thing is worth remembering, though, and it's that those vows you made, 'for better for worse, for richer for poorer, in sickness and in health' apply to both of you … you can't (you lazy, greedy minx) decide that you took him 'for richer, for better, in health', while reserving all the easy options for yourself, 'poorer, for worse, in sickness'.

And you might care to remember that you are both still the same people you were before you married. If he was a beer-swillin', sofa-huggin' X-box obsessed fella before, he still will be now, whatever your expectations of a husband may be. It goes without saying that you're still the disco dancin', shoe buyin', ciggy lovin' gal you were too … so don't let him (matri)moan if he wants you any other way. Yup, the things we overlook in our haste to be wed can often be the things that drive us firstly insane and secondly apart. But let's remember that all relationships, not just marriage, are hard and need to be worked at, and with divorce being notoriously messy and stressy, isn't it worth closing our eyes to each other's little foibles, and aiming to stay wed?

MARITAL (DISTANT?) RELATIONS

We've established that you've made your matrimonial bed. But now you have to lie in it … forever! You might wonder how on earth you'll manage this, when many modern newly weds claim they're too tired, too drunk or having too much 'real fun' to even have sex on their wedding night. But the fact is, as we marry later in life (probably after having lived together for umpteen years), we're hardly likely to be virgin brides and grooms, champing at the bit to get to each other's, um, bits. Yes, whereas in the past the first bedtime of marriage was something to look forward to, the climax, if you will, to the main event, in these times of ever-more elaborate dos, the best we can hope for is a quickie pencilled in between the canapés and the cake.

But it doesn't have to be like this, my horny honeymooners! There are plenty of ways to make this evening go with a bang, even if you've both been around the block more times than Michael Schumacher. Why not, for example, agree to add a new string to your sexual bow on this special night or, if you're too exhausted, for the honeymoon? Maybe a new position, technique or tantalising toy you've both wanted to try, but have shied away from in the past[75] – anything that will put the spice into getting spliced and have you blowing each other's minds, as well as everything else. If you're short of ideas, anal sex could hit the (g) spot if you've never partaken before. But do discuss this in advance, as he might put a red light on your desire for changing lanes and find it more alarming than alluring!

Whichever naughty novelty you choose, there is certainly a lot to be said for starting your married life together filled with lust as well as love. But just how long can we realistically keep up (ho ho) our desire for one another? The average marriage now lasts roughly eleven years, probably about the same amount of time it takes for passion to die and mutual disgust or apathy to set in. Library and bookstore shelves are fair weighed down with tacky tomes entitled 'Staying in Lust with the Same Person for the Rest of your Entire Life Even Though You're All Too Familiar with their Revolting Personal Habits'.[76] Such books usually

---

75 Don't worry, you'll be merrily filled with booze, which will help with those pesky inhibitions – but best not to try anything involving delicate hand-to-eye co-ordination or operating machinery!

76 Before you rush out to buy this book, it does not exist; I am being satirical, see? Although maybe an idea for my next oeuvre …

dole out plainly bonkers advice to keep you and your husband, well …
bonking: ogling porn together, for example, role-playing or getting
dressed to thrill.[77] It's a personal choice, of course, whether these appeal,
or have you running for the hills for the nearest chastity belt.

But maybe you would go even further to keep the spice in your sex life?
Perhaps as far as the Macgregor's suburban bungalow for a spot of
swinging? For, according to recent reports, swinging among middle-
aged couples is on the increase, which can be considered in one of two
ways (although let's not get up too close). Perhaps it's lovely that
married couples in their golden years are 'beavering' away to keep the
love alive? Or, what's wrong with the good old-fashioned way of doing
things: affair; bitter argument; kiss and make up; reciprocal affair;
bitter divorce. Indeed, some couples may even feel that affairs are the
only way to keep the marriage going and agree on an 'open marriage',
which sounds great if you can manage to keep the human emotion of
sexual jealousy out of things. But, surely there must be a better way of
keeping things fruity with your spouse?

Well, listen up, my libidinously lacking ladies, and listen well!
Perhaps the answer isn't to go to any lengths to increase our sex drives
when they are naturally on the wane. Perhaps we should just accept
that, for many of us,[78] partying naked becomes less of a shag fest with
each passing decade. I mean, we don't hang our heads in shame and go
running for reassurance if we become less active in any other area
pleasurable area of life. We simply say, 'That was a nice trip to the
theatre/scuba diving expedition/visit to the crafts fair, I must do that
more often', without any need for crying on girlfriends' shoulders or
psychoanalysis. That's not to say we should give up on sex altogether,
which would be a crying shame. Nope, we should keep our legs open to

---

77 Of course, whether you indulge or not will depend upon your political stance regarding pornography.
   For some, it is perfectly okay and titillating, but for others it is the exploitation of vulnerable women, as
   well as the objectification of women in general. A debate too complex to have in this bijou footnote.

78 I say many of us, because I don't deny the principle of the (s)exception proving the rule.

our spouses, as well as all channels of communication, but let's just not act like bunny boilers if we're not at it like rabbits!

Suffice to say, no matter how hard we try, sometimes a marriage will turn sour and there is nothing we can do to sweeten it. But let's not end this book on a bad note, and go for a happy ending instead! For the time has come for me to a bid you a fond farewell in the postscript that follows. In the meantime, good luck, my married maidens, may yours be one of the ones that lasts!

Modern Dilemma

Dear Modern Maiden,

I've taken on the responsibility of being Maid of Honour at an old friend's wedding next summer. I say old friend, not in the sense that we have been lifelong best buddies, but that we were extremely close as children and have had little to do with each other since (we are in our twenties). I took on the role as I did not want to let her down, but now it seems she is going to delegate all sorts of responsibilities to me, from being the main contact with the caterers, to ordering all the decorations for the church. I thought my primary function was simply going to be to cop off with the dishy best man. I feel like resigning from my position, but how can I let my friend down gently?

Yours despairingly,

Debbie

Dear Maid of Dishonour,

If I may be so bold, what kind of friend are you? You say you've had little to do with each other during your adult years, so your friend must think back on the childhood times together as something pretty darned special. Or, she hasn't made any good friends since … either way, having agreed to the role she wants you to play, you can't back out now just because it seems too much like hard work. On the other hand, do you really deserve to have first dibs on the pretty best man, with such an ugly attitude? I suspect your friend would think rather not …

Yours tisk-tiskingly,

MM

Dear Modern Maiden,

For months now I've been planning my fairytale wedding to the boy I've long thought of as my one true love. But recently I bumped into an old flame and, as we got chatting, I realised my feelings for him were more of a raging inferno, than dying embers. He asked me to go for a drink with him next Saturday night, two weeks to the day before my wedding. I am in a real pickle over whether to go … my head says no but my heart is aflame.

Name withheld

Dear Got-Yourself-in-a-Pickle,

So, you want to have your (wedding) cake and eat it too? It's very common to have cold feet before your Big Day, but this sounds to me like you're frozen all the way up to your nose! Only by meeting him will you be able to tell if your head and heart are going to be in agreement, and if they are, you must inform your betrothed and his closest family face to face. And before the wedding itself — t'would be most unladylike to jilt him at the altar.

Yours fondly,

MM

POSTSCRIPT

A FINAL WORD IN YOUR EAR

There we have it. I hope you've come away from this book feeling you've had a bit of fun, learned a few new tricks, and found some food for thought to boot.

Mostly though, I hope that we can now wholeheartedly agree that it's time for the rise of Modern Maidenhood: that it's time we lasses put two fingers up to the nanny state, and make the mistakes we'll inevitably make along the way. It's time we wore the trousers in society (albeit beautifully tailored ones – natch), and most of all, it's time that we realised we can get on in life simply by being ourselves, without being told what to do. Go get 'em, my most Modern Maidens!

ACKNOWLEDGEMENTS

Thank you firstly to everyone who anonymously contributed stories and offered support, especially to my sister Pony de la Mer for reading, commenting on and (occasionally) laughing at some of the chapters, all the girls at booze – or rather book – group, as well as Rehana Ahmed, Rosie Nixon, Jo Blackmore, Sarah Maynard and Kristina Schulz. Biggest thanks (and love) to my husband, Roly Allen; he's not a Modern Maiden but after the amount of time he spent reading (and improving on) the endless drafts of this book, I think he's entitled to honorary membership. And if I may waffle on in gratefulness a little longer, I'd like to thank my editor, Barbara Phelan for all her useful comments, ideas and and of course for commissioning the book in the first place! I'm also very grateful to Barbara for finding Jo Hayman who did the gorgeous illustrations and cover. Last but not least, Barbara and I would like to thank Julie Burchill for writing such a splendid and witty introduction. Drinks – and anything else you fancy – are on me, everyone!